St. Paul

ST. PAUL

An Urban Biography

BILL LINDEKE

MINNESOTA
HISTORICAL
SOCIETY PRESS

Cities, like people, are always changing, and the history of that change
is the city's biography. The Urban Biography Series illuminates the unique character
of each city, weaving in the hidden stories of place, politics, and identity that
continue to shape its residents' lives.

Unless otherwise noted in the caption, all photos from MNHS Collections.

mnhspress.org

The Minnesota Historical Society Press is a member of the
Association of University Presses.

Manufactured in the United States of America

10 9 8 7 6 5 4 3 2 1

♾ The paper used in this publication meets the minimum requirements
of the American National Standard for Information Sciences—Permanence for
Printed Library Materials, ANSI Z39.48–1984.

International Standard Book Number
ISBN: 978-1-68134-200-9 (paper)
ISBN: 978-1-68134-201-6 (e-book)

Library of Congress Control Number: 2021938176

This and other Minnesota Historical Society Press books are
available from popular e-book vendors.

Contents

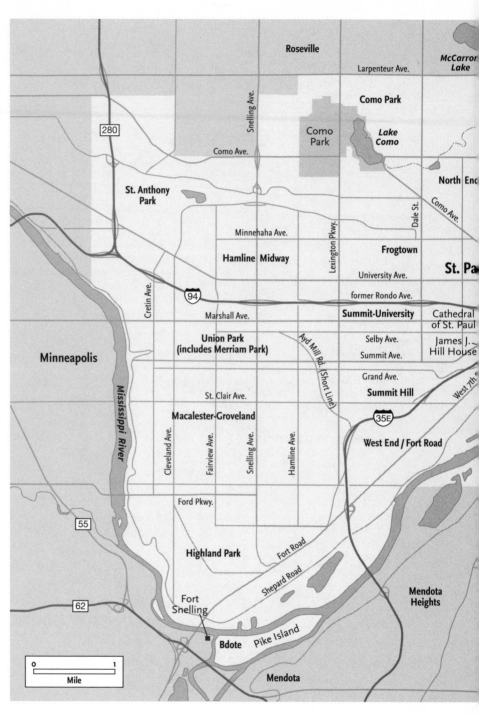

Map by Matt Kania, Map Hero Inc.

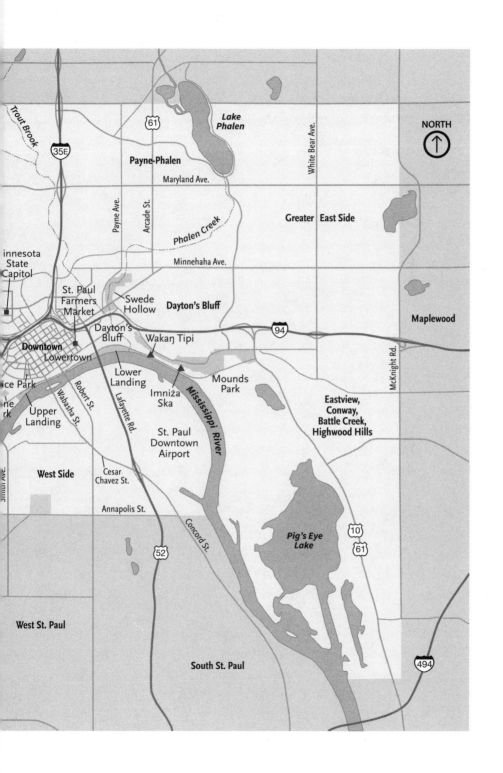

Prologue

When my mother was pregnant with me, my parents lived in an apartment on St. Paul's West Side, just blocks from the bluff with the city's best view. My father's family has been in St. Paul for five generations, dating back to the territorial days, but my mother is from Canada. In those early years, I was told, she was learning to be a proper St. Paulite, someone who knew the difference between Phalen and Como, who understood why it makes perfect sense that the West Side was in the south.

To love St. Paul is to hold in your heart indignant pride about such things. When my mom went into labor, my dad was not pleased that doctors told him to drive her to Fairview Hospital, which was in Minneapolis. "Minneapolis?" he supposedly fumed. "No child of mine is going to be born in Minneapolis!" He caved on that particular point, but the sentiment certainly pervaded my childhood. We were always proud of being from this city, and I was trained to take great offense at slights: for example, releasing an exasperated sigh if an airline pilot should welcome passengers to the "Minneapolis airport."

Growing up like this, crossing from the West Side over the Smith Avenue High Bridge, which stretches rather precariously over the Mississippi River bluffs, was always an event. "Good ol' St. Paul, there it is," my father would say as we dropped down the bridge. The view is spectacular, and the city opens up like a pop-up book: Summit Avenue mansions nestled among the trees on the hill, while downtown appears like a vision at the bend in the deep river valley.

The only time we willingly went to Minneapolis was for Twins games or an occasional visit to a museum. There was nothing else we needed over there, in a city with weird high-brow pretensions, where even the meticulous way the streets were arranged seemed wrong. Something about the street signs was overbearing, and the modernism of places like the Guthrie Theater or Orchestra Hall, even to young eyes, seemed like it was trying way too hard. St. Paul, on the other hand, was comfortable, historical, and down-to-earth. This was a town that balanced nicely between the future and the past. As my dad might have said, if you couldn't do it in St. Paul, it probably wasn't worth doing.

But the stories we tell ourselves about where we live erase as much as they reveal. Consider the public art in St. Paul's glorious 1932 City Hall and Ramsey County Courthouse, built in the midst of the Great Depression. In the heart of the skyscraper sits the wood-paneled council chamber, a high-ceilinged room with brass pillars framing an art deco clock whose hands slowly thunk their way around the dial, the city's obscure seal hanging on the opposite wall. To decorate the chamber, the architects hired a Chicago muralist named John Norton to create four large paintings. Well-lit, colorful, and twenty feet tall, the four monumental artworks were intended to depict the story of St. Paul. All of them feature a white man towering over a moment in city history. In one, a woodsman holds a canoe paddle in a forest; in another, a steamboat captain looms over men working on the riverfront. On the other side of the room, a land surveyor stands somberly before the setting sun, steadying a theodolite with his right hand; next to him, a factory worker in overalls leans while carrying a wrench, looking wary of whatever comes next.

But at the margins of the murals, other figures appear. In one scene, two Native American men stand in front of a US military soldier holding a sheet of paper. In another, a Native man paddles a canoe carrying a fur-hatted frontiersman with a gun. A Catholic priest holds a cross before a pair of Dakota men. Elsewhere, two Black men trudge onto a steamboat, heavy bags slung over their shoulders. Next to the feet of the massive factory worker, a Black railroad porter carries luggage for a

well-dressed white couple stepping off a steam train. The woman following her companion is the only female anywhere in the set of paintings.

Unwittingly or not, the murals reflect one reality of the city's development. St. Paul's history was dominated by white men, wealth, property,
and capitalism, while the consequences for others were often troubling
or traumatic. To give but one example, the same year the murals were
installed, federal housing inspectors arrived in town with their clipboards,
examining urban neighborhoods for slums and racial integration. They
wound up redlining huge parts of St. Paul, dooming the people who
lived there to generations of disinvestment.

For decades, these massive murals framed the city's leaders as they
made critical decisions, and they loomed over the public as they gave
testimony or witness to their local government. But as the twenty-first
century began, more people began to notice these paintings, focusing
particularly on what they revealed and what they omitted. Community
activists and historians alike called for alternative stories and symbols,
hoping for public art that better reflected the city's complex history, values, and people.

After years of community lobbying and intense discussions about
the past, city and county leaders decided in 2018 to cover the paintings
and replace them with new artworks. By 2020, even as St. Paul was
in the midst of political turmoil and a raging pandemic, new paintings
were mounted on the walls. The new murals tell other stories, and the
plans call for changing these artworks over the coming years to bring
even more of the city's history to light.

The history of the city is one thing, but the history of this place is
a much longer story. For centuries before the name "St. Paul" had ever
been uttered, this land was the heart of the Dakota homeland. It remains
so today, and for that reason a history of St. Paul will always be limited by
a fundamental erasure. There is a growing literature on Dakota history
and culture, and readers who pursue it will likely find that it changes
their perspective on what it means to live in this city and this state. This
book, an urban biography of St. Paul, will always be predicated on that
colonization, and the countless ways that American power was used

to displace the Indigenous communities who lived here. In that story, St. Paul plays a special role as a center of the political system that forced out Dakota and other Native people.

For better and for worse, this is a story of St. Paul, a name that carries a legacy of displacement and decades of unequal struggle. My own personal experience, and that of my family, leads me to look from a specific point of view, as part of a community who mostly benefited from the city's uneven landscape. My perspective is full of fond memories of exploring the city's nooks and crannies, the odd parks, forgotten diners, fancy restaurants, delightful delis, and aging alleyways.

There are surely many other stories to tell. There's the 1965 Daylight Saving Time fiasco, when for ten days the clocks in Minneapolis and St. Paul were an hour apart. There are the competing origin stories for the name of "Frogtown," the neighborhood where I now live: according to the family schism, it earned its moniker either due to the prevalence of wetland chorus frogs or due to early French-speaking settlers. There's the story of Amelia Earhart's two years at Central High School, when she sought refuge at St. Clement's Church to escape her troubled parents. You might learn about the invention of the revolving barber pole, or the paper bag with handles, or the pop-up toaster. Or you can learn about the last remnant of forgotten Lafayette Park, on the far eastern edge of downtown: an oak tree from 1826 still stands over the parking lot where the neighborhood used to be.

None of those stories are in this book, but they're all worth learning. The more we make the time for sharing our countless tales, listening to those of others, swapping histories, riddles, and tragedy, the more we can learn to love the place that is St. Paul.

CHAPTER 1

Naming

Below Fort Snelling, seven miles or so,
And three above the village of OLD CROW?
Pig's eye? Yes; Pig's eye! That's the spot!
A very funny name; is't not?
Pig's Eye's the spot, to plant my city on,
To be remembered by, when I am gone.
Pig's Eye, converted thou shalt be, like SAUL;
Arise and be, henceforth, SAINT PAUL!

—James Goodhue, *St. Paul Pioneer,* January 1, 1850

Walk to one of St. Paul's fine promontories, gaze on the landscape, and you will see the Mississippi sweep through the curving bluffs of a wide valley, flowing south to the Gulf of Mexico. The city sits on sublime, uneven geography, the land formed by millennia of glaciers, rivers, and creeks carving through bedrock. The result is a geology of bluffs, valleys, and even a hollow or two surrounding a hilly plateau in a broad river bend. Unlike Minneapolis's flat landscape to the west, where the prairie begins, St. Paul's uneven topography is that of a prototypical river city, a place defined by its Mississippi banks.

Ten thousand years ago, if you had looked out from the bluffs, you'd have seen an astonishing sight: an arcing waterfall, larger than Niagara, carrying a rush of water south from a massive glacial lake. About two hundred miles to the northwest, the melting ice age glaciers had formed an enormous lake on the plains, which emptied through a massive river that carved the Minnesota River valley. A few miles upstream, where the two rivers came together, the Minnesota River carried far more water than the smaller Mississippi flowing from the north. This glacial torrent carved the wide valley where St. Paul sits today.

5

It is crucial to remember, always, that the city grew at the heart of the homeland of the Dakota people, who had thrived in the Minnesota and Mississippi River valleys for thousands of years before Europeans and Americans arrived. St. Paul's birth grew from a sometimes-violent mix of settler colonialism, exploitation, tribal conflict, political rivalry, and dispossession, much of which centered on the politics and machinations taking place in the future capital of Minnesota.

The most visible traces of the area's long Dakota history rise on the bluffs on St. Paul's East Side, where the oldest human structures in the city appear in the form of burial mounds overlooking the valley. The mounds sit high over the white sandstone cliffs just downstream from today's downtown and were once more common in and around the river bend, but today only six remain. Archaeologists believe the mounds were built two thousand years ago, part of what they call the Hopewell culture, named for the Ohio farmer in whose field one of the burial sites was first excavated. Similar mounds once stretched from the Canadian border to Louisiana. Many were burial sites, and others were constructed in the shapes of animals. Many Dakota people simply say that the mounds were built by their ancestors and continue to view them as sacred places, a central feature of the Dakota homeland for millennia.

The different names used to describe places reveal a relationship among social groups, memory, and the environment. From one perspective, names suggest boundaries, property, or Christianity; from another, a name can invoke spirituality or long histories that connect people to place. Lucien Galtier renamed this bend in the river St. Paul, inscribing a foundation of settler colonialism and providence for this city on the Mississippi. But for thousands of years before, and still today, this place has been and remains the Dakota homeland. Called Imniża Ska, the place with white cliffs, it is part of Bdote, the confluence of the Mississippi and Minnesota Rivers, and encompassed by Mni Sota Makoce, the land where the waters reflect the clouds.

The Dakota people are one of seven groups known as the Oceti Sakowiŋ (Seven Council Fires). The nation—known to Europeans and Americans as the Sioux—is generally divided into two halves: the Eastern Dakota, who lived and hunted in the forests and savannas along the upper and lower Mississippi, Minnesota, and St. Croix, and the Western Dakota, who lived and hunted on the plains to the west. The word *bdote* means "confluence," and the confluence of the two great rivers carries special significance: it is a sacred meeting ground for Dakota from near and far. The rivers offered convenient routes for gathering to trade furs, food, goods, and stories. For some Dakota people, the bdote is the spiritual center, the spot where the Dakota came down from the stars. It remained so even as Ojibwe, Europeans, and Americans began to arrive from the East to trade and meet at Bdote in ever larger numbers, and it remains so today.

The Dakota who lived near Bdote were of the Bdewakaŋtuŋwaŋ band, the easternmost group, and life revolved around seasonal patterns and change. Most Dakota lived in large villages along the rivers during the summer, planting crops and hunting game. In the fall, they harvested wild rice from lakes and made trips around the region, sometimes venturing onto the plains to hunt buffalo. In the winter, Dakota people formed small family camps in sheltered woods, organized around game and fishing. In the spring they stayed at the sugar bush, harvesting maple syrup before returning to their summer villages. Each year the pattern continued, through droughts and floods and cold and warm winters, and language and stories evolved along with the slowly changing landscape of connecting rivers, the lakes to the north, and the prairies and big woods full of game. In the middle of it all, the bend in the river by the white cliffs under the burial mounds offered a great location. Near a small valley through which a brook flowed south from the lakes over the hill, a band of Dakota people led by a number of chiefs named Little Crow had a summer village called Kaposia on the river's lowlands.

The first European to pass through this place was most likely Father Louis Hennepin, an explorer and Catholic missionary who ventured up the Mississippi River in 1680 on a trip to explore what he called New France. This massive territorial claim, made a few years earlier by the French, followed the European Doctrine of Discovery, by which European Christians claimed for themselves any lands not subject to other

Lith Jnat Arnz & Cᵒ Düsseldorf.

Kaposia as depicted by artist Henry Lewis, who saw it in 1848

European Christian monarchs. Hennepin's group was trying to discover the mythical Northwest Passage when they ran into a group of Dakota people. As Hennepin described it, they were kidnapped by a war party, but it's just as likely that the Dakota sheltered them for about a year as guests, helping out these mysterious strangers. By either account, Hennepin passed through what is now St. Paul on his way up the Mississippi River, before turning north to Mille Lacs. Afterward, as the fur trade flourished in what is now Minnesota, French voyageurs and traders interacted with the Dakota people in the area around St. Paul.

Following the American revolution, European land claims east of the Mississippi River were transferred to the United States, whose plans to expand westward into Native American territory were fundamental to its new national identity. As part of that effort, an American military explorer named Jonathan Carver visited the Dakota village in what would eventually become St. Paul in 1766. Carver's visit is famous today for his description of a cavern he "discovered" in the bluff, "a remarkable

The Fur Trade

Over a century before Zebulon Pike arrived at Bdote seeking a site for an American fort, Dakota families had traded for European goods like kettles, knives, cloth, and guns with other Native nations like the Ojibwe and the Meskwaki (Fox), who acted as intermediaries with whites. Tribes to the north were more easily accessible for European trade via the Great Lakes and other waterways, and the fur trade was controlled by a handful of French and British public or private monopolies. In Dakota territory, the early trade was often more complicated. French traders had difficulty establishing stable trading posts, and instead many Dakota dealt with *coureurs des bois* (French for "runners of the woods"), unlicensed French traders who often married into tribal communities and worked as individual entrepreneurs.

Over the years of the trade, the French and British influenced Dakota relationships by trading weapons directly with the Dakota or arming rival tribes to the north or east. In this way, access to European goods altered the balance of power within the Mississippi River valley. At the same time, to the dismay of the French and British, much of the fur trade in Dakota territory was not strictly for profit. Instead, trading furs or food for goods was just one among many strategies for providing for people in the village each year. Historian Mary Lethert Wingerd described this tension: "The French—and the British and Americans who followed them—tried their best to enmesh the Indians in an acquisitive culture of consumption, which would then impel them to put all their energies into hunting for the trade. However, to the continuing frustration of the Europeans, the Indians refused to embrace the profit-making ethos that was central to the European mindset." The trade thus became part of a struggle between Indian values of kinship and American frontier capitalism, a tension that intensified over the decades.

In the years following the Louisiana Purchase, American companies took over the fur business and established formal relationships with Dakota tribes. The Dakota traded at posts established on waterways, exchanging furs, wild rice, and other foods for goods from European or American suppliers. The American Fur Company post at Mendota (an anglicization of Bdote), across the river from Fort Snelling, served as a trading center from the 1820s to the 1840s.

By the 1830s, the trade was in decline. European hatmakers who had demanded beaver fur shifted their interest to more fashionable silk. Game was becoming scarcer as the population at Fort Snelling grew, but more importantly, after the establishment of Wisconsin Territory in 1836, the land itself was becoming valuable to speculators. This includes the area that would become St. Paul, changing the delicate dynamics of Native labor and exchange. Native communities with heavy debts and poor food supplies could be persuaded to relinquish land for annuities, and these payments wiped out long-standing debts, allowing traders to cash out. By 1840, the best years of the fur trade were in the past, though it remained a lifeline of resources and income for Dakota people for decades afterward.

cave of amazing depth" that would eventually bear his name on American maps. For the Dakota people, that cave is known as Wakaŋ Tipi, the Dwelling Place of the Sacred, intimately connected with both Bdote and the spiritual power of water.

Decades later, when an army officer named Zebulon Pike arrived at the rivers' confluence in 1805, it was a turning point for what would become St. Paul. Pike had been tasked by the US Army with securing locations for military posts, which would keep British fur traders out of the area claimed in the Louisiana Purchase. Visiting Bdote, Pike met with Dakota leaders, including Little Crow (the father and grandfather of later leaders by the same name), who was then living at Kaposia. In a gathering on the island at the rivers' confluence, Pike persuaded the Dakota chiefs to sign a document that the Americans claimed granted acres of land for the construction of a military fort. Because the Dakota concept of land was fundamentally different from European definitions, the chiefs likely had a different understanding of the treaty, though they were eager for consistent trade with Americans. Even American accounts of the land agreement were dubious; Pike left the amount of compensation blank

Sketch of Pig's Eye Parrant, made about 1892

on the document, eventually writing in an admittedly low sum of $2,000. When he brought the document back to Washington, the treaty was never fully ratified by Congress, and the treaty's sum was not paid to the Dakota for fifteen more years.

In 1819, the US government dispatched one hundred members of the 5th Infantry Regiment to build and staff a fort, and construction began on a spot high on the bluff overlooking an island where the two rivers met. Soon afterward, in 1823, the first steamboat successfully navigated the difficult straits at Rock Island, bringing trade from the south into the Dakota homeland. From that point on, the American military was a fixture at Bdote, and the fort served as the critical spot for diplomatic and trade relations with both the Eastern Dakota and the Ojibwe people to the north.

Oddly enough, most of the first white people who lived in what is now St. Paul did not come from the east or the south, along the later path of European migration, but from the north. In the 1820s and 1830s, dozens of French, Swiss, and Scottish people fled a remote settlement located at what is now Winnipeg, Canada, coming south to the new American fort. The distant settlement was founded by Thomas Douglas, the Fifth Earl of Selkirk, who was "granted" a large tract of land in the center of British land claims. At the time when the first colonists reached the site, in 1812, it was many weeks distant from other towns or trading posts, surrounded by Cree, Ojibwe, and Dakota lands. From the European perspective, it was the end of the known world, and the settlement was heavily disliked by fur traders, who opposed its colonial presence.

Somehow Selkirk's European pitchmen had convinced hundreds of Swiss and Scottish emigrants to follow the earl to the distant plains of present-day Canada and begin farming, but when they arrived, the group struggled in one of the most ill-fated settler colonial projects of the nineteenth century. The prairie winters were brutal, and summer for the Selkirkers was not much better. The settlement was beset by years of floods, fires, plagues of grasshoppers, and other hardships, all while residents were being harassed by fur traders.

After years on the brink of starvation, groups of Selkirkers began abandoning the colony in the mid-1820s. They headed for the closest white settlement they could find, trekking south to the new American fort at the Minnesota and Mississippi Rivers, named by then for Josiah Snelling, its first commander. Snelling and Major Lawrence Taliaferro, the Indian agent who represented the US government at the fort, welcomed the settlers to live on the military reserve, where they could raise crops and livestock to provision the soldiers. They set up camp a short distance away, near a site called Mni Sni by the Dakota and Coldwater Spring by the military.

The fort's Canadian refugees were grateful to be connected to some semblance of European settlement, and to see the first-ever steamship reach the confluence, loaded with supplies, must have seemed miraculous. As river traffic increased over the next few years, both the refugee settlement and Fort Snelling grew, creating a diverse mix of peoples. On any given day you might find Dakota, Ojibwe, Swiss Selkirkers, white soldiers, and fur traders of French or mixed heritage. For years, the community also included enslaved men and women serving the military officers, including Dred and Harriet Scott, who were married at Fort Snelling in 1837. The Scotts would later, unsuccessfully, use this time spent at the fort in the ostensibly free North to justify a claim to freedom in the infamous 1857 Supreme Court case.

By the time of the Scott wedding, the social landscape around the Upper Mississippi and St. Croix valleys was changing quickly. Game was becoming scarcer, and the fur traders, turning to other occupations, were often illegally harvesting timber for firewood and construction, without permission from the Dakota. In some parts of the St. Croix valley, small logging crews were already shipping logs downriver to St. Louis, while American authorities like Taliaferro rarely did much to enforce the boundaries of tribal sovereignty. The impact of dwindling resources limited the options for Dakota and Ojibwe people, and many tribal leaders began to sign treaties opening land for settlement in the hopes that federal annuities would help them survive. Taliaferro, in particular, worked to get funding that he believed would provide stability for the

Dakota, operating under the assumption that they would give up their way of life and take up farming. Under treaties signed in 1837, land east of the Mississippi and south of a line running through Mille Lacs Lake, including most of today's St. Paul, was opened up for logging, land claims, and the rest of the changes that came with American settler colonialism.

It was at this point that, anticipating a rush of land speculation, military leaders at Fort Snelling worked to clear the military reservation of civilians. When the polyglot refugees who had been permitted to live near the fort were kicked out, they moved across the river to stake their claims on the eastern side, land they thought was now open for settlement. Their new cluster of cabins, claims, and homes, dubbed Rumtown, sat along the banks of the Mississippi, near a stream in what is now Hidden Falls Regional Park in St. Paul's Highland Park neighborhood. The Rumtown settlers, who often made a handy living trading whiskey, proved to be a huge thorn in the side of Taliaferro and the fort's commanders. Drunkenness was a perennial problem at the fort; particularly during the interminable winters, soldiers had little to do but drink, carouse, and fight.

With the impending signing of treaties with Dakota and Ojibwe nations, and land speculation in the air, Taliaferro and other fort officers knew well that land claims east of the Mississippi were an opportunity. They used vague rules over what constituted the fort's "unorganized territory" as a way to ensure their chance at the richest claims. In 1839, Major Joseph Plympton, the fort's commanding officer, persuaded the federal government to expand the reservation boundaries to include land on both banks of the river, arguing that the timber was required to sustain fort business.

The new boundaries meant that the Rumtown settlers would need to move, and that October, Plympton sent troops to Rumtown to evict them. Perspectives vary on how the day went down: Taliaferro claimed that the eviction was peaceful, while the settlers reported that the soldiers set fire to their cabins and destroyed their property. By either account, the first non-Native St. Paulites had been rudely displaced, and had to find somewhere else to ply their wares and stake their claims.

It was at this point that a famous St. Paul legend begins, as refugees wound up following an odd trailblazer. Pierre Parrant was a French Canadian fur trade veteran known for trading whiskey and skirting the edges of the law. Parrant, called Pig's Eye because of a facial deformity, built a cabin next to a large cavern along the Mississippi named Fountain Cave, downstream from Rumtown and just past the new boundaries of the military reserve. He spent a year there peddling whiskey to Dakota people, soldiers, and anyone else who came along; the cave served as a convenient hiding place for his still. A year later, in 1839, when he again lost his land due to ongoing debt problems, he simply moved downstream.

The 1837 treaty had given him an option. When the Dakota ceded land on the east side of the Mississippi River, the Dakota community at Kaposia, near the base of the mounds bluffs, moved across the river to the flats in today's South St. Paul. Parrant built a home at the lowlands just upriver from Wakaŋ Tipi. This time the location worked out, and Pierre Parrant became the first white resident in the community that would become St. Paul.

Forced from Rumtown and the fort's margins, a dozen settlers soon joined Parrant at the river landing, creating a small village at the bend in the river. Parrant's saloon and the surrounding village sat on a spot central to early Mississippi River traffic near the head of practical navigation. It quickly became a convenient place to stop for supplies or to enjoy some of Parrant's whiskey, as one traveler did one day in 1839. A French Canadian carpenter named Edmund Bisset was in Parrant's tavern writing a letter to an acquaintance on downstream Grey Cloud Island. Amusing himself, he filled out the return address as Pig's Eye, starting a running joke for the settlers at the river landing. When the reply was delivered to the new address, the village had a name, sometimes rendered as Pig's Eye's Bottom. Parrant himself did not much enjoy the nickname and eventually lost his claim, vanishing into the northern Wisconsin forest sometime in 1842. But Pig's Eye's legend became St. Paul's colorful origin story, told in bars and back rooms around town to this day.

Drawn from remembrance of a physiognomist.

PIERRE PARRANT, OR "OLD PIG'S EYE."

Sketch of Pig's Eye Parrant, made about 1892

Fountain Cave as drawn by an anonymous artist, about 1850

The Pig's Eye story fits with the common narrative of ostensible Minnesota progress. Then and now, these stories pit a debauched, "uncivilized" past against a subsequent wave of refinement and accomplishment. In the nineteenth century, this narrative was typically fixated on the Dakota people, who were doomed, in the parlance of the times, "to disappear before the settlement of the white man" and fade into history. Early depictions of white settlement in Minnesota, such as the paintings by Seth Eastman, typically feature one or two Native Americans in the foreground, with the new buildings and white settlement featured in the center of the frame, forming a hierarchy of the marginalized. Likewise, the Minnesota state seal, adopted in 1858 and still in use (in modified form) on the state flag, tells the same tale: a Dakota man on a horse riding into the sunset while a settler farmer plows a field, his rifle tellingly within arm's reach. The story of Pig's Eye Parrant offers a similar before-and-after scene, a morally ambiguous, racially polyglot past cleansed through religion, temperance, and refinement as the city grew. This is how the early St. Paulites chose to see

Seth Eastman's graphite drawing of St. Paul, 1848

themselves—as salvation for an immoral frontier outpost, a redemption story.

In St. Paul's case, the redemption became official with the arrival of a French Catholic priest. Increasingly in the 1840s, riverboats stopped at the small village on the landing on their way to the fort, often to unload their supplies of whiskey barrels. In 1840, a Catholic priest named Father Lucien Galtier was one such visitor to Pig's Eye village on his way west. Based in Prairie du Chien, Wisconsin, Galtier received a warm welcome from the many Catholic French-speaking settlers, who hadn't seen a proper priest in years, if ever. Galtier even got two village residents to donate land to erect a chapel at the center of the settlement. It was a small log structure with a small wooden cross, and Galtier named it the Chapel of St. Paul. From that point, the growing village, which had dozens of citizens intent on civility, began using "St. Paul's landing" or "St. Paul's" instead of Pig's Eye to talk about themselves. The name stuck.

Most Americans and Europeans arriving in St. Paul in those days were drawn by one of three things: land speculation, profiting through the "Indian trade," or missionary work. People often got involved in all three, and for many St. Paulites, whiskey was the problematic commodity that lay at the intersection of it all. Whiskey was a prized possession in frontier St. Paul, while at the same time, its heavy use flew in the face of both the authorities and the missionaries. For example, Taliaferro, the head Indian agent until 1840, was a teetotaler, and he worked tirelessly to keep whiskey out of Dakota territory. At the same time, demand for whiskey was tremendous, and many men in early St. Paul made their living exploiting this gap and evading the law.

The 1837 treaties, championed by Taliaferro, were also a boon to the early St. Paul economy, bringing large sums of federal money into the territory. While the annuities were intended to help the Dakota and Ojibwe, their corrupt administration meant that white traders made healthy profits off annual payments. By the 1840s, the long-established fur trade was near its end because, increasingly, land was becoming more valuable to the invading immigrants for purposes other than trapping.

As land was ceded, Native hunters were less able to repay their debts with fur, and traders like Henry Sibley, the head of the American Fur Company post just across the Mississippi River in Mendota, increasingly turned to Native annuities as an income stream. When payments arrived from Washington, DC, the traders were often first in line to get a cut of the money; the fur trade became the Indian trade. For example, Henry Rice, a fur trader and Indian agent, and Henry Sibley's longstanding partner and rival, built a small fortune out of annuity payments intended for the Ho-Chunk people (who were moved to Minnesota from Wisconsin in 1846). He later bought up many of the best land claims in early St. Paul, investing wisely and becoming the town's biggest booster. He dedicated the city's first park and built the first hotel in town, becoming a champion for the interests of the new settlement.

Though Pig's Eye Parrant gets the credit for being the city's first resident, there were many other early settlers with equally compelling cases. There were people like Vital Guerin, a stubborn former fur trader who donated the land for Galtier's chapel, and later gave away a large portion of his claim to another French Canadian trader just to have some company. James Thompson, another early settler, was St. Paul's first Black resident. In the 1830s, a Methodist missionary named Albert Brunson purchased Thompson from the army officer who enslaved him, then freed him so he could serve as a translator. Married for years to a daughter of Dakota leader Maȟpiya Wiċaṡṭa (Cloud Man), Thompson had learned the Dakota language well. Thompson worked at Kaposia with Brunson, who was trying, almost always in vain, to convert the typically uninterested Bdewakaŋtuŋwaŋ Dakota to Christianity.

Perhaps fed up with Brunson's cultural insensitivity, Thompson left the mission in 1839 and moved to Rumtown to sell whiskey before being displaced along with the rest of the settlers. Shortly afterward, he moved to a shanty near Parrant's claim, and for years he ran the ferry that crossed the Mississippi River. In one tale, typical of the time, Thompson got into a fight with the settlement's most combative Irishman, Edward Phelan, who had stolen Thompson's prized pig without apparent provocation. After Thompson triumphed at fisticuffs, they shared a drink together and, according to Phelan anyway, "ever after . . . [they] were good friends." The prickly Irishman would later infamously star in the city's first murder trial. In 1839, Phelan was accused of killing John Hays, his roommate at the time. The trial was a sensational ordeal, but Phelan was acquitted. For some reason, a creek and lake still bear a version of his name.

The inelegant challenges of early St. Paul didn't stop people like Harriet Bishop, the most famous of St. Paul's early Protestant reformers. Bishop arrived in town from New England in 1847, in response to desperate pleas sent east by early St. Paulites, begging for a schoolteacher. Bishop wrote two popular accounts of her struggle to redeem the morals of the new settlement, one focused on her efforts to open St. Paul's first school, and the other on the US–Dakota War of 1862. Bishop was less than charitable when describing the St. Paul she found in 1849, writing that the town was nothing but "some half dozen decayed and decaying log hovels, chinked with mud, and every way of the meanest appearance, evincing the lack of taste and ambition in the occupants."

In the early 1840s, St. Paul was still the closest white population to the Selkirk Red River settlement, across the British border far to the northwest. The Red River colonists had survived the worst years of assorted plagues and floods, and now there was money to be made providing trade goods to the Red River Valley. Fur trader Joe Rolette had first shown this in 1821, when he famously had his employee Alexis Bailly drive a herd of cattle four hundred miles north, from St. Paul's landing to the distant colony, where they sold to the Canadians at record prices. Similarly ambitious St. Paul middlemen began turning a lucrative profit on the trade between the two settlements, and from the 1830s until 1872, when the railroad reached the Red River, all roads led to St. Paul. Trains of oxcarts would string from St. Paul on one of three Red River trails, and the long lines of carts impressed early settlers when they arrived, a few times a year, on the bluffs near today's Cathedral Hill. The drivers were figuratively and literally colorful, dressed in flamboyant outfits and scarves, and almost always part of the Métis community at Pembina in Dakota Territory—people of mixed Ojibwe, Cree, and French descent

Red River Half-Breeds and Carts.
(Upton's Series of Minnesota Views.)   No.
For BEST VIEWS, go to Martin's Art Gallery, 264 Third-st., St. Paul.

Red River oxcarts in downtown St. Paul, 1858. *Photo by Benjamin Upton*

who had a unique language and culture and a centuries-old practice of commercially hunting buffalo. Oxcart trains were made up of dozens or even hundreds of two-wheeled carts formed from wood and bison hide that squeaked loudly, especially when loaded with half a ton of furs or dry goods. Many of St. Paul's early elite, men like Norman Kittson and Henry Sibley, added to their fortunes by supplying the distant colony with goods.

The other big pillar of the early St. Paul economy was land speculation. While many early land claimants in St. Paul were simply looking for places to live, by the late 1840s Minnesota was inching closer to becoming a territory. As Wisconsin became the country's newest state in 1848, any man with enough capital, like Kittson and Rice, could make a fortune flipping land claims in the new village. Speculation pressure grew even hotter in 1849 thanks to some political gamesmanship during the federal territorial negotiations. Jockeying for position, the territory's most influential early leaders crafted a gentlemen's agreement: St. Paul would become the territorial capital, St. Anthony (the future Minneapolis) would get the state university, and Stillwater would get the state prison. In all cases, the federal spending was the big prize, and local boosters in each settlement, often sunk deep into debt by land purchases, craved these lucrative contracts. Once St. Paul became the territorial capital, though only on a temporary basis, real estate prices shot through the roof.

Meanwhile, the fledgling town had a neighboring community, just six miles downstream. When the leader—who, like his father, was known as Little Crow—died suddenly in 1846, his son Taoyateduta (His Red Nation, later also known as Little Crow) arrived to take over leadership of the band. Taoyateduta, the younger son, had been living with Dakota relatives to the west, along the Minnesota River, and when he and his entourage arrived in their canoes, he found that his brother was also claiming village leadership, and was not too happy to see him arrive. In response, Taoyateduta challenged his brother, who then shot him with a rifle. Though the bullet pierced both of his wrists, he survived; the village, impressed with his bravery, acclaimed him chief.

For the next fifteen years, Taoyateduta became a regular visitor to the streets of St. Paul, to trade or visit with the European Americans. Taoyateduta was a keen observer of the fast-growing town of St. Paul, watching the steamboats pass by the village, the newcomers gawking at the sight of Dakota homes and people. As steamboat traffic increased, and more and more people began arriving in St. Paul, the new town would become the fulcrum for transformation on the Upper Mississippi.

CHAPTER 2

Dispossession

Saint Paul['s] . . . new frame buildings, glistening with the reflection
of the rising sun, imparted to it an air of neatness and prosperity. . . .
Everything here appeared to be on the *high pressure* principle. A dwelling
house for a family could not be rented. . . . We are now near the dividing
line of civilized and savage life. We can look across the river and see
Indians on their own soil. Their canoes are seen gliding across the
Mississippi, to and fro between savage and civilized territory. They are
met hourly in the streets.

—E. S. Seymour, travel writer, 1849

Winters in early St. Paul likely seemed longer than anyone reading
this can imagine, and not just thanks to climate change. Mississippi
riverboats were the literal lifeline for the town, providing the people,
news, and supplies on which settlers depended. When the river froze
each November, becoming impassable, St. Paul's pace slowed to a crawl.
People bunkered up or left, and the wintertime population was a fraction of its summer size. Mail from St. Louis, Chicago, or Washington
might be delivered only once a month, a fact that particularly bothered
the restless civic boosters. To get word from the East, dogsled teams used
the frozen Mississippi as a dangerous path to the south, or else traveled
overland on a rough, long "road" through western Wisconsin to the nearest river outpost, La Crosse.

But everything changed each spring, when the ice broke apart and
the first steamboat came up the river. The arrival meant St. Paul would
be connected once again to the rest of the fast-growing country. It was,
as one observer remarked, "the town's greatest holiday of the year." The
anticipation was especially keen in the spring of 1849, as St. Paul's eight

hundred residents had waited impatiently all winter for word on their
official status. Henry Sibley, the longtime fur trader and leading citizen, had spent the winter in Washington negotiating the passage of a
bill that would make Minnesota an official territory—a declaration that
came with all kinds of federal perks and guaranteed a steady stream
of immigrants. All through the cold months, nobody knew whether or
not they would be a territory until one day, on April 9, the ice broke up
and the steamboat *Dr. Franklin, No. 2* chugged around the bend in the
Mississippi. It arrived, no doubt tooting its own horn, while half the
town gathered around the lower landing to hear word from the Capitol.

For St. Paul, it was good news. Sibley had succeeded in a close nego-
tiation in Congress, then embroiled in debates over the expansion of
slavery, and Minnesota had officially become a US territory. Alexander
Ramsey, a Pennsylvania politician, was appointed governor. This was
music to the ears of the boosters with land investments and growth
schemes on their minds, which described pretty much every immigrant
at the time. For the next few decades, the city would double in size repeat-
edly, to thousands in 1855, ten thousand in 1860, and twenty thousand
in 1870. Yet in early days of the territory, the path of growth was not set
in stone. Settlement depended on making connections to the east and
the south along the Mississippi River, and using those connections to
take the land from the surrounding Dakota nations.

On any given summer's day, a visitor could take the pulse of St. Paul
at the riverboat landings. The larger "lower landing" sat close to the spot
where Pig's Eye first built his saloon, near the corner of today's Jackson
Street and Shepard Road, the low point that rose to the higher land in
town. Early St. Paul spread out from there, along the cliffs overlooking
the river, rising over the hills where homes were protected from spring
floods. A small "upper landing" sat a half mile upstream, where Chest-
nut and Eagle Streets meet the Mississippi today. As the city grew, the
upper landing began to serve the booming communities around Seventh
Street, then the western edge of town.

Between May and November, the two river landings bustled with activity, and on any given day there might be one or a dozen boats at the dock.

The riverfront swarmed with men loading and unloading crates full of goods and with immigrant newcomers speaking a half dozen languages, hauling suitcases to the nearest hotel, which was almost always full. Men made good livings orbiting the landings, refueling boats with firewood, connecting visitors with lodgings, or (better yet) bilking newcomers out of any savings brought to the booming frontier.

For a time, the west side of the Mississippi remained Dakota land. As boats full of migrants steamed into St. Paul, they passed by the relocated site of Kaposia village, where South St. Paul now sits. Invariably, the arrivals rushed to the port side to gaze at the bark huts, tipis, and rows of corn, and to marvel at the supposedly backward ways of the Dakota. For their part, the Dakota at Kaposia, like their leader Taoyateduta, may have gazed back at passing boats full of people hungry for land. The booming population fueled exponential growth in land prices and added huge pressure to increase settlement. Minnesota's leaders schemed to

Steamboats *Grey Eagle, Frank Steele, Jeannette Roberts,* and *Time and Tide* at the lower levee, 1859

get the Dakota to "sell" their remaining land. On the one hand, traders floated goods on credit, anticipating government payouts in the future; at the same time, existing land rights and annuities were not well enforced, so that Dakota people rarely got what they had been promised and had to continually chase scofflaws from the west side of the Mississippi.

Territorial authorities usually ignored complaints from Dakota leaders about poaching, trespassing, or timber theft. In 1851, facing few good choices and intense pressure from Governor Ramsey, the fur trade agents, and white settlers, Taoyateduta and other Dakota leaders signed the Treaty of Mendota at Oheyawahe, or Pilot Knob, a sacred Dakota site on a hilltop overlooking the rivers' confluence. With this treaty and another signed the same summer at Traverse des Sioux, the Dakota were forced to surrender thirty-five million acres of what is now southern Minnesota, retaining narrow strips of land along the Minnesota River, in exchange for annuities and promises.

The treaties of 1851 also meant big paydays for Indian agents and anyone involved in the Indian trade, and they kicked off the biggest era of land speculation in Minnesota history. When the treaties were signed, men like Henry Sibley, Henry Rice, and Norman Kittson, longtime fur trade veterans, were first in line to receive payments for debts alleged against Native people. The debts were so large that, much of the time, the Dakota, Ojibwe, and Ho-Chunk people received only a small fraction of the promised payment. In addition, the annuities meant a huge boost to the cash-starved frontier economy. As the *Minnesota Pioneer* reported on August 8, 1850: "One would suppose by the promises about town, that the Indian payment would square every debt in Minnesota, but the 'debt of Nature.' Every reply to a dun is, 'after the payment.'"

Opening all of southern Minnesota, most of the Dakota homeland, to white settlers and speculators induced a frenzy. By 1852, St. Paul was reeling with real estate deals, as one visiting journalist described: "My ears at every turn are saluted with the everlasting din of land! land! money! speculation! saw mills! land warrants! town lots, &c. &c. I turn away sick and disgusted. Land at breakfast, land at dinner, land at supper, and until 11 o'clock, land; then land in bed, until their vocal organs are exhausted—then they dream and groan out land, land! everything is artificial, floating." The frenzy for land stretched from St. Paul down the Minnesota River valley, and claims on new townsites were swapped like trading cards. A claim bought in St. Paul for thirty dollars might sell for ten times that amount a year later, and with prices like that, few could resist getting in on the action. New suburban neighborhoods like Irvine Park (still existing) and Lafayette Park (now a parking lot) popped up on the edge of town like flowers in the spring. In fact, the oldest remaining house in St. Paul dates to this time, a small home built in 1850 by a steamboat captain from Missouri not far from the upper landing, near stately Irvine Park.

Land speculation forms the backdrop for St. Paul's most famous early political stories, still told in the back rooms of Ramsey County. Though St. Paul had been chosen as the territorial capital back in 1849—a plum that came with ample federal spending—that status had been temporary. At any point, the territorial legislature could decide to change it, and the speculative politics of land grabs and boosterism made the decision a highly political one. Nearly everyone in territorial Minnesota had a stake in boosting the price of some land, somewhere, and the decision about the new capital was a key political plum. For example, one influential citizen, Henry Rice, had spent heavily on buildings and land plats in the heart of St. Paul. Naturally, Rice tried his damnedest to keep the capital located near his investments.

But other Minnesota forces had schemes of their own. In 1857, a group of politicians with land investments in St. Peter, a hundred miles up the Minnesota River valley, made their move. The group's members included Governor Willis A. Gorman, and using their connections, they passed a bill through the legislature pledging to move the capital from St. Paul. Rice and other St. Paul speculators were incensed. They persuaded a legislator named Joe Rolette to abscond with the printed copies of the bill from the floor of the legislature and hole up with them in a nearby hotel. For the next few days, the county sheriff "tried" to look for him, but Rolette, a cantankerous fur trade veteran from Pembina, ran

Alexander Ramsey House / Irvine Park

In the late 1860s, Alexander Ramsey, Minnesota's first territorial governor, built an elaborate, mansard-roofed mansion along Exchange Street on what was then the western edge of St. Paul. The house, designed in the French Second Empire style, was erected from the Platteville Limestone distinctive to pre-railroad St. Paul. Ramsey, who had become quite wealthy by the 1870s, insisted on the latest state-of-the-art technology, which included radiators, gas lights, and hot water. Ramsey and his family lived there for decades, and his grandchildren occupied the house into the 1960s, when it was donated to the Minnesota Historical Society to serve as a historic site. The building is also a reminder of Ramsey's legacy: he was the architect of the treaties that took southern Minnesota from the Dakota people, and after the US–Dakota War of 1862, as the state's governor, he called for their extermination or expulsion from the state.

The Ramsey House sits on the edge of Irvine Park, St. Paul's last intact pre-1880s neighborhood, one of the handful of Victorian upper-class residential districts that once sat at the fringes of town. Built before streetcars fueled the wider growth of the city, upper-class neighborhoods were a short walk from downtown's booming warehouses and industries. Similar enclaves elsewhere in the city, like the Central Park and Lafayette Park neighborhoods, steadily declined and were eventually demolished for parking, roads, or development.

By the 1950s, tiny Irvine Park, sitting in the shadow of the downtown bluffs, did not seem salvageable. As planners and developers floated ideas to demolish the buildings for parking or housing complexes, community organizing in the West Seventh Street neighborhood and historic preservation efforts kept the planners at bay. Instead, over the next ten years, many homes were moved to the area from elsewhere in the city, in an attempt to consolidate and save St. Paul's historic housing stock.

Today the area offers the best collection of pre–Civil War and Victorian homes in the city, including a small square park with an elaborate fountain dating to 1881, a replica of the original. The Irvine Park neighborhood reveals a glimpse into what a nineteenth-century bourgeois community might have looked like, well worth a trip for visitors to downtown St. Paul.

Alexander Ramsey, right, in a carriage outside his home in Irvine Park, about 1900

out the legislative clock, allegedly playing cards and drinking whiskey. He reappeared at the capitol just after the final gavel fell, and so St. Paul remained the capital after all.

Just as it does today, St. Paul hosted many of the state's political fights, which were, at times, both figurative and literal. In the 1850s, the territory's political balance was dead split between the Democrats and fledgling Republicans. The former dominated the older settlements along the Mississippi River in the southeast and in the north, and the Republicans and lingering Whigs claimed the west and south as strongholds. St. Paul became the battleground for heated disputes over everything from railroads to abolition to Native annuities to the state's eventual borders. The town's newspapers, saloons, and hotels were constantly hopping with political argument and debate. After one particularly nasty session, a newspaper praised the decorum of territorial legislator (and future governor) William Marshall: Marshall had not violated "the dignity and rules of the house by knocking [fellow legislator Henry Jackson] down while the body is in session. He waited for the adjournment before he did it."

Temperance was another hotly contested political issue, and especially so in St. Paul, a place that, as Mark Twain said, was formed and led by "the jug of empire." The city was infamous for its prodigious pace of booze consumption. The whiskey question heated to a boil when, for a few brief months in 1851, led by moral reformers in nearby St. Anthony, pro-temperance forces gained a slim political majority. With the help of reform-minded Catholics, they passed a so-called Maine Law banning alcohol in the territory. In St. Paul, where nearly every business profited from whiskey sales and nearly every resident regularly imbibed, the prohibition was both reviled and ignored. When a territorial judge threw out the law on a technicality, as recounted by temperance missionary Harriet Bishop, the whiskey-loving folk of St. Paul rejoiced: "On the night of the repeal, a large steamboat bell was mounted upon wheels and attended by scores of miserable human beings, went booming through the streets of the capital, proclaiming death to temperance principles, and loud hurrahs for the movers of repeal."

Politics changed quickly in St. Paul thanks to the steady arrival of migrants from the East. The newcomers dramatically bolstered the territorial population and brought with them a multitude of religious and political convictions. At the time, more and more newcomers were German speakers, typically liberals fleeing the failed Prussian and Austrian revolutions of 1849. They arrived in St. Paul throughout the 1850s, bringing with them ideas of political reform, antislavery tendencies, and brewer's yeast for making lager beer, a staple in Bavaria but rare in the Northwest. The German communities transformed the political landscape of Minnesota and made it all but impossible to imagine passage of another prohibition law. German communities formed throughout St. Paul, especially in the West End, near Smith Avenue and West Seventh Street, where you can still find some of the city's oldest breweries. Writing in 1875, an early city historian described the German speakers "as among our most 'solid' and well-to-do citizens, owners of fine business blocks, and comfortable residences, and gratifying bank accounts."

For some in St. Paul, boosterism and profit got in the way of moral concerns like the question of slavery. Because of legal changes surrounding the status of those who had escaped slavery and fled to free states, in the 1850s it became technically legal for southerners to bring enslaved people on travels to the North. Burgeoning St. Anthony and its new neighbor across the river, Minneapolis, were already famous by then for their New England culture, and the presence of accompanying slaves proved quite controversial. Groups of abolitionists picketed the southern slaveholders, sometimes trying to "rescue" the enslaved as they stayed in hotels.

In St. Paul, on the other hand, Democratic business leaders maintained an uneasy political relationship with the South. While not as passionate as its western neighbors, St. Paul was still the northern terminus of steamboat traffic, and smuggling runaway slaves via the underground railroad was a time-honored tradition. With the aid of abolitionists, three of the city's Black barbers, well-respected residents of the town, helped dozens of escapees pass through St. Paul on their way to British territory and freedom. As the nephew of one of them later recalled, "I can't tell how many slaves we got away, but we were so industrious that the slave owners gave up bringing their slaves with them, when they came up here, long before the war."

At the same time, St. Paul businessmen tried valiantly to keep abolition politics at bay, especially after the financial crash of 1857 devastated the local economy, by ensuring a steady flow of wealthy southern visitors to the city's hotels. At one point during the 1860 legislative session, St. Paul representative Charles Mackubin proposed legalizing slavery in the state, but only between the months of May and October, the peak of southern tourist season. Thankfully, the bill did not pass.

St. Paul's slavery tensions boiled over that same summer when Henry Sparks, a "body servant" owned by a southern tourist named Martha Prince, was liberated—told he was technically free—by Black workers at a St. Paul hotel. He walked away in the middle of the night, but his recapture by St. Paul police triggered an outcry. The testimony of the Black eyewitness to the armed capture, a St. Paul man named John Freeland, was later refuted by the city's police chief and mayor, both of whom testified that the authorities were not there. The court found Freeland in contempt, and Sparks was returned to the woman who claimed to own him.

As the Civil War raged in 1863, another incident found a community of families escaping slavery in Missouri and fleeing north to St. Paul. The group was led by a determined freedom seeker named Robert Hickman, and together they escaped their captors, built a makeshift river barge, and began to paddle up the river to freedom. Their river craft proved to be unmanageable, and when they began drifting south, the captain of a passing steamboat called the *Northerner* took them in tow. Hitching the raft and its seventy-six passengers to his stern, the steamboat brought them to what he thought would be safe haven in St. Paul.

When the inhabitants of Lowertown—the part of the city surrounding the lower landing, often called New Dublin for its preponderance of poor Irish wage laborers—saw the raft full of Black people arriving, a riot nearly broke out. As a newspaper described at the time, "the police were very much alarmed at the appearance of such a thunder cloud, and thinking they were to be landed here, proposed to prevent it on the ground that they [Hickman and his followers] were paupers. The Irish on the levee were considerable excited, and admitted by their actions that the negro was their rival, and that they fear he will outstrip them." The *Northerner* towed the escapees instead to Fort Snelling, where they were welcomed onto the free soil of Minnesota. For the newcomers, it helped that the Civil War had put pressure on the local labor market, and the military needed workers.

Years earlier, through most of the 1850s, St. Paul had been booming. In those years, merchants sold goods at nearly any price, and everyone in town counted on rising land values to foot the bill for the inflationary wares. As one historian described it, "Emigration was pouring in astonishingly, several boats landing daily loaded with passengers. Those intending to go back in the country, usually purchased their supplies here [in St. Paul], and the stores were almost overtaxed, so profitable was their trade. The hotels and boarding houses were crowded to overflowing. . . . That season they coined money. . . . The city was continually full of tourists, speculators, sporting men, and even worse characters, all spending gold as though it was dross."

The speculative fervor came to an abrupt halt in the summer of 1857, when the Ohio Life Insurance Company went bankrupt, triggering a run on every bank in the country. Almost everyone in St. Paul lost a fortune overnight, from the paper millionaires to the working stiffs suckered on

St. Paul, 1857. Workmen build the new county jail at the corner of Cedar and Fifth Streets, in the foreground; the dome of the Methodist Episcopal Church at Jackson and Ninth is at top center. This photo is part of a panorama shot from the roof of the first courthouse, at Fourth and Wabasha.

land deals. To make matters worse, the city's population, boosted by years of get-rich-quick schemes, plummeted by half. Every bank in St. Paul failed, making it all but impossible to find bank notes to make a business transaction.

After the crash, St. Paul was a different city. The boomtown that was the central trading point, political headquarters, power center, and supply depot for thousands of new migrants looking for cheap land changed. For the merchants, boosters, and speculators who profited from the frenzy, as buildings rose along the city's dirt streets like weeds, it all came to a halt that summer.

The next few years brought long winters and low morale. It took St. Paul nearly a decade to slowly crawl back toward solvency, especially given the tumultuous politics of the day. In the meantime, the national Republican landslide election of 1860 led to not one but two wars for Minnesota. The first, the Civil War, saw 1,400 St. Paulites, a large portion of the town, volunteer or get drafted to fight for the Union Army. Some were enthusiastic about the idea, and others, particularly the Irish, less sanguine about dying for the cause. Draft officials entering St. Paul's Irish Lowertown had to bring armed guards, and even they did not stop anti-war Irish women from retaliating, in one case, by dousing the officials with washing water.

St. Paul played a far larger part in the second big war, the US–Dakota War of 1862. The conflict profoundly shifted the identity of the city away from the older fur trade veterans who had made their living in "the trade," exploiting the power dynamics between the federal government and the Dakota, Ojibwe, and Ho-Chunk tribes. The old traders had stayed ahead of shifting political winds sweeping into the state, but the thousands of new settlers who had arrived in the 1850s dramatically altered the landscape as they went west to take land near the Dakota reservation. Many of the new arrivals spoke European languages and were baffled by Native American cultures. They also tended to vote Republican, supported more harsh treatment of Native people, and increased the pressure on both the Dakota and Ojibwe.

In fact, anti-Native political pressure was commonplace in young St. Paul. In one high-profile case, a Dakota man named Yuhazee was hanged in 1854 in front of a public crowd on what is now Cathedral Hill, overlooking the city, for killing a German woman in the Minnesota River valley. A few years later, St. Paul found itself amidst a fiasco called, somewhat derisively, the Cornstalk War. Just before the financial crash of 1857, facing incidents of conflict between settlers and Ojibwe to the north, an early city militia was formed to keep the peace in the region. Goaded to "do something" about the Natives, who had been stubbornly leading their lives as they had for hundreds of years, some St. Paul leaders sent a poorly trained and inexperienced militia north to confront a small Ojibwe hunting party in Chisago County. The resulting confrontation did not go well; gunfire was exchanged, and one Ojibwe man and one white man from St. Paul were killed. After some chaos, the militia reported to the authorities in St. Paul with five Ojibwe captives.

At the time, many men in St. Paul leadership were fur trade veterans who had long experience dealing with Ojibwe people. When they found out what had happened, they were horrified. They quietly released the captives, allowing the supposed shooter, a man named Shagoba, to escape. The mayor even enlisted Joe Rolette, fluent in Ojibwe relations, to take the wronged men for a night on the town. Rolette treated the men to dinner and snuck them into a theater show as an apology for the fiasco.

By 1862, after years of neglect and broken promises by the US government, violent conflict had broken out a hundred miles southwest of the city. Starving Dakota people, led by Taoyateduta and the Bdewakaŋtuŋwaŋ Dakota who had formerly lived in the villages around Bdote, attacked white settlers farming in the Minnesota River valley. The Dakota killed more than six hundred settlers, including children, while an unknown number of Dakota people were also killed. The killings out west inflamed anti-Native sentiment in St. Paul, leading to calls for genocide. The lurid stories of "slaughter on the prairie" reinforced long-held insecurities about so-called "savage Indians" as a threat to settler prosperity. The fury in the city grew deafening, and St. Paul newspapers frothed

with various calls for retribution or blood. One demanded "a war of extermination against the Sioux savages," and state officials offered bounties
of up to $200 to anyone who killed a Dakota person.

The city's residents soon had a chance to witness the pain of the
Dakota who surrendered, including people who had sheltered whites
and opposed the fighting. In the winter of 1863, a plot of land at Bdote,
at the foot of the bluff below Fort Snelling, became the site of a con-
centration camp for the Dakota women, children, and elders, who were
separated from their husbands, fathers, and sons. About 1,600 Dakota
people were confined there before being shipped up the Missouri River
to a new reservation on arid land. In hasty trials organized by Henry
Sibley, 265 Dakota men were condemned to death. When President
Abraham Lincoln refused to hang all but thirty-eight of the Dakota, the
district attorney published an "open letter from the citizens of St. Paul"
castigating the decision. For decades afterward, Taoyateduta's remains
were displayed at the Minnesota Historical Society's library in the state
capitol. And for generations, this tragic moment of Minnesota history
was held up as justification for the colonization of Dakota land.

While the Dakota War solidified the colonial narrative in St. Paul,
the Civil War bolstered the new state's identity as a part of the larger
nation. At the same time, years of bumper crops and inflated wartime
commodity prices meant that St. Paul merchants were finally making
money again after the '57 crash. With the economy on the rise, city leaders turned to the next big push: getting a railroad into the city. A railroad
connection to the East or the South would end the seasonal instability
that came with reliance on the Mississippi River for trade. A railroad
would connect St. Paul to the booming states of Iowa, Wisconsin, and
Illinois, and all the immigration and money that came with them.

But building a railroad to distant St. Paul was not easy. During the
boom years, all kinds of schemes were in play. Territorial leaders tried
desperately to deploy land grants to get a rail connection to Dubuque,
Duluth, or Chicago, but each of the schemes ended with the '57 crash,
and the war years threw all plans into limbo. Despite it all, St. Paul leaders
managed to complete ten miles of track between St. Paul and St. Anthony

in 1861, beginning the transformation of the town's riverfront dynamics. A new locomotive called the William Crooks was shipped by riverboat that year. When it began service, it cut freight costs between the two cities in half, and slowly the ambitiously named St. Paul and Pacific Railroad began expanding. From its initial ten-mile line to St. Anthony, the railroad extended its routes over the years to towns like St. Peter, Shakopee, and Stillwater. But the city still lacked a railroad to Chicago or Dubuque, and the economic holy grail—a transcontinental line linking St. Paul to the booming resources of the untapped territories between Minnesota and the West Coast—remained a distant dream.

The Pacific connection would take a lot more time and financial scheming, and it became the main topic for business rivalries that played out over the postwar years. No one in town proved better at the cutthroat railroad game than a young Canadian Scot named James Hill. He had arrived in St. Paul just before the crash of '57, when he learned a valuable lesson about booms and busts on the settler frontier. Hill was working on the docks at the age of eighteen, loading goods into warehouses, but his education and penmanship quickly earned him work as a clerk for town grocers. Meanwhile, the 1860s were full of fierce competition for railroad development, especially for the valuable land grants that accompanied the successful completion of a new line. But the difficulty of construction meant there was a long list of failed St. Paul railroad ventures, including no fewer than four state-sponsored endeavors that failed following the '57 crash. When a railroad went under, the rights to bankrupted railroad grants were forfeited and could be bought for pennies on the dollar, an opportunity for some other entrepreneur or sucker to try to lure investments from eastern banks to a Minnesota railroad.

Hill, for his part, spent those years saving money and rising up the ranks of the merchant business class, eventually becoming a warehouse and wholesale entrepreneur in his own right in 1866, right around the time St. Paul began to experience the postwar business boom. Boosterism was the name of the game, and the more railroads a town had running through it, the more wealth it could generate with raw materials and real estate investment. Hill managed to get exclusive shipping rights for

An engine at the levee, about 1870. Railroads would make steamboats nearly obsolete.

the new railroad that connected to his docks in Lowertown, linking shipments of goods like flour, wheat, and lumber to the markets down the river. Along the way, he met and married a young Irish waitress named Mary Mehegan—a match that would prove to be pivotal for St. Paul history—and built a house in the bourgeois neighborhood on the northern edge of downtown.

By 1869, St. Paul railroads had reached Sioux City, Iowa, and Morris, Minnesota, just as investors in Duluth were hatching their own plans for the first transcontinental route to the West. That ambitious effort was the brainchild of a Philadelphia financier named Jay Cooke, who had invested heavily in railroad connections to Duluth, which he envisioned as the next Chicago, eclipsing St. Paul altogether. Meanwhile, St. Paul railroads reached Chicago by 1872, putting the capital at the center of a rail network stretching throughout Minnesota to Canada and Dakota Territory. It remained an open question which railroad would be the first to reach the Pacific, bringing wealth to its investors.

Nobody knew that another financial bust lay just around the corner. In 1873, waves of financial speculation and leveraged investments broke and triggered a panic, starting with Jay Cooke's railroad investment company, which collapsed. The crash triggered another wave of financial depression and bankruptcies in Minnesota, and this time the young James Hill was prepared to take advantage. Hill formed a partnership with his friend Norman Kittson. Drawing on connections he had made

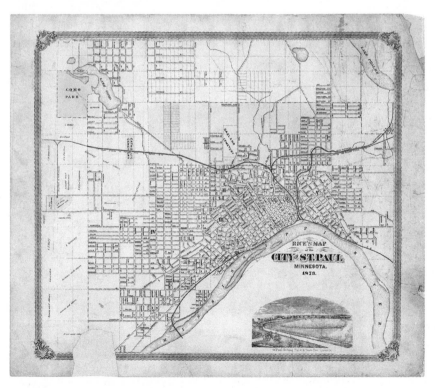

Rice's Map of St. Paul, 1873. The city's western boundary is Lexington Parkway.

on an 1870 dogsled journey to the Canadian border, he secured capital from a Montreal bank. According to the agreement, Hill would operate as a front man, and together they used Canadian capital to acquire the rights to the bankrupt railroads running north and west into grain country.

In 1878, Hill and his partners convinced Dutch bankers, fed up with the lack of return on their Minnesota holdings, to sell them the rights to Cooke's entire enterprise. Hill then began his campaign as the leading railroad builder in Minnesota. Within a few years, thanks to bumper grain crops and an economic rebound in Minnesota, Hill's newfound rail monopolies had become immensely profitable. He leveraged the proceeds into transcontinental expansion, and by the fall of 1883, the Northern Pacific line was complete all the way to Tacoma and Portland. The streets of St. Paul hosted a grand celebration. The new line boosted the

On September 3, 1883, St. Paul celebrated the completion of the Northern Pacific's line to the West Coast with a massive parade that passed down Third Street (now Kellogg Boulevard). They were greeting Henry Villard, president of the railroad, and US President Chester Arthur, who were on their way to drive the last spike.

city economy and transformed the old Lowertown neighborhood into a railroad boomtown full of warehouses, merchants, and suppliers of every stripe. St. Paul was at the center of a vast network connecting the cities of the Great Lakes to the frontier and the booming Northwest. It seemed all but certain that St. Paul would grow into the next midwestern metropolis destined for greatness.

CHAPTER 3

Boomtown

St. Paul is a wonderful town. It is put together in solid blocks of
honest brick and stone, and has the air of intending to stay. . . . It is a
very wonderful town indeed, and is not finished yet. All the streets are
obstructed with building material, and this is being compacted into
houses as fast as possible, to make room for more—for other people are
anxious to build, as soon as they can get the use of the streets to pile up
their bricks and stuff in.

—Mark Twain, *Life on the Mississippi*, 1883

In 1889, work began on James J. Hill's new Summit Avenue mansion.
The railroad tycoon was at his peak of wealth and power. The Great
Northern, Hill's own transcontinental railroad, which Hill proudly declared would be built entirely with private funds, was to run through the
obscure Marias Pass in the Montana Rockies on its way to Washington
State. To be completed in a few years, it would connect St. Paul to the
Pacific Ocean. At this point, Hill controlled both the Northern Pacific
and the Great Northern, giving him immense power to shift the fates of
trade, settlement, speculation, and tourism. All along the way, Hill funded
the construction of towns and businesses connecting St. Paul's merchants to the distant hinterlands. By consolidating Minnesota's rail net-
works, Hill ensured that St. Paul, not Duluth or Minneapolis, would be
the primary terminus of the northwestern network, thereby keeping the
city's businesses thriving. His massive new house cemented his place
in the city's topography as its richest and most influential citizen.

If you wanted to make a statement in booming St. Paul, there was
no better place to build a mansion than Summit Avenue. The street ran
along the crest of the bluffs to the west of downtown, and any home

Construction crew for James J. Hill's mansion, about 1891

built on the edge was always on full display to the townsfolk below.
A few years before, Summit Avenue had been little more than prairie
wilds, a convenient camping spot at the edge of town for the Red River
oxcarts of the Métis.

But the new northwest railroads made the oxcarts obsolete, and Summit Avenue was destined for opulence. Within a short time, St. Paul's
new elite built grand palaces along the boulevard, literally rising above
the hoi polloi. Summit quickly transformed into the premier mansion
district, where the city's richest families flaunted wealth in the stone turrets, balconied porches, and gardens of dozens of Victorian mansions.
High on the bluff, men like Hill literally looked down on the valley
below, the dirty city thriving with the smoke of locomotives, factories,
and warehouses, boasting a tumult of boats, wagons, railroads, and the
people fueling Minnesota's rapid change.

St. Paul's greatest boom began in the late 1870s, as the city worked itself out of yet another financial panic. Nourished by the railroads, warehouses and factories popped up throughout the city. The railroads meant a steady stream of wheat from the Red and Minnesota River valleys and lumber from the north coming into St. Paul to be shipped downstream. In turn, the city's merchants supplied the frontier with all types of goods, manufactured in St. Paul or imported from the East. Banking, insurance, small manufacturers, and warehousing grew to meet demand, employing the migrants that streamed into the city, the vast majority of them white Europeans: Germans, Irish, Swedes, Norwegians, Czechs, Slovaks, Russian Jews, Italians, Scots, Swiss.

The wave of immigration tripled St. Paul's population from forty thousand in 1880 to over 130,000 ten years later, and the city kept growing. By 1910, St. Paul boasted 214,000 residents, an explosive rate of growth that transformed the landscape in all directions. New neighborhoods were continually platted at the edge of town, streets laid out through the old woods, each vying to be the next destination for the middle classes. Once the first horse-drawn streetcars were constructed in the 1870s, settlement began filling in the open land between the city and far-off Minneapolis. St. Paul was changing from an intimate, walkable river town to a booming midwestern city of railroads and streetcars at the heart of Minnesota.

To fit the growth, St. Paul's first shift in its borders lay south across the Mississippi River. In 1859, when the city was only five years old, engineers constructed its first bridge over the Mississippi. It was an awkward-looking steel affair perched over a river island, linking the top of the downtown bluffs to the low-lying flats of what was then West St. Paul, a separate city in Dakota County. Because the bridge funding was provided by St. Paul and Ramsey County, to recoup expenses they levied a toll for crossing, a fee that remained irksome to the people on the other side. To get rid of the toll, in 1874 the two sides forged a deal: Dakota County let St. Paul and Ramsey County annex the northern, urban part of its domain in exchange for removing the toll. There was only one catch: Philip Crowley, an Irish immigrant and the superintendent of

Union Depot

In St. Paul's early railroad years, each line had its own separate station, used for both passengers and freight. As traffic increased, a new Union Depot was constructed in 1881, to combine the various passenger stations into a single place serving the vast majority of passengers. Rebuilt after a fire just three years later, the large brick station towered over Fourth Street in Lowertown, on the edge of the city's commercial and retail district. On any given day, dozens of passenger trains arrived and departed from the depot, carrying travelers and luggage arriving from all over the country, while friends, families, porters, and maintenance crews all bustled about.

After another fire destroyed most of the building in 1915, a modern new Union Depot was funded and completed, opening in 1923. As both the Great Northern and Northern Pacific railroads were based in St. Paul, the large neoclassical edifice was constructed to reflect St. Paul's status as one of the country's railroading centers. In those years, the city's most famous trains—the Zephyr, the Hiawatha, and the 400—could each make the 430-mile trip from St. Paul to Chicago in just over six hours, far faster than Amtrak today. They pulled into the depot throughout the day on one of the ten rail platforms, and the station was the beating heart of the city, connecting it to the greater world. It bustled with people at all hours of the day and night, hosting shops, restaurants, and even a bowling alley inside its walls. The depot also served as a US Postal Service station, handling the third-largest amount of mail in the country.

St. Paul's passenger rail traffic peaked during the late 1920s at 275 trains a day, before gradually declining as buses, airlines, and personal automobiles competed for trips. When Amtrak was formed in 1971, consolidating the nation's remaining passenger lines under public ownership, St. Paul's passenger rail service moved to a small unadorned station in the Midway industrial area. Without the trains, the depot's massive waiting room was sealed off and purchased by the US Postal Service. The front lobby housed a series of restaurants, including one of the first-ever Leeann Chin locations and Christos, a long-lived lunch spot serving Greek food. Meanwhile, some of the depot's office space became loft condos overlooking the streets of Lowertown.

In 2011, using federal funding, Ramsey County bought the building and began an elaborate $240 million effort to restore the depot to its 1920s condition and—given its proximity to the planned light rail line—turn it into a multimodal transportation terminal. Crews spent a year repainting and rehabbing the depot, reopening the waiting room and bringing trains back to Lowertown. The restoration crew unearthed small details like the bas-relief murals and old clock lettering, and they restored the original yellow and green paint colors.

Unfortunately for rail fans, the depot hosts only one passenger train a day in each direction: the Empire Builder, which runs from Chicago to Seattle and is named after St. Paul's own railroad baron, James J. Hill. While county and state officials plan on someday bringing more passenger trains back to the station, on any given evening you might find the waiting room hosting an event, a wedding, or a market or simply serving as a place for people to walk around and pass time in the heart of downtown St. Paul. If you're very lucky, you may even see people getting off a train.

Dakota County Schools, had a farm north of the proposed boundary on Annapolis Street. The new county border would make him a Ramsey County resident; facing the prospect of losing his lofty position, Crowley found a third choice. A compromise agreement carved a forty-acre notch from the new city boundaries, neatly around his property. The odd boundary line remains to this day along St. Paul's southern border. Then as now, St. Paul was not keen on letting the perfect be the enemy of a good deal.

Without the bridge toll, the population of the low-lying land across the river began to grow. Known as the West Side Flats, the neighborhood became an affordable enclave for the diverse immigrants arriving in the city. In the early days, Irish and German immigrants lived on the flats, but by the 1880s the area was home to hundreds of Russian Jews fleeing czarist persecution. Speaking a handful of languages, St. Paul's early Jews built at least three synagogues on the flats, where they lived in ramshackle, hand-built homes alongside immigrants from Lebanon,

Wabasha Street Bridge, about 1870

Ireland, Bavaria, and many other parts of the world. As folks found steady jobs and scraped up savings, families moved up and away from the flood-prone river and onto higher ground. On St. Paul's uneven geography, the hills were for the rich and the rivers and ravines housed the poor, topography that made class stratification both a figurative and literal reality.

In addition to growing at the margins, St. Paul's development moved outward alongside the new railroads linking to Minneapolis and out-lying towns. By 1882, for a small fee you could ride to Minneapolis in twenty-five minutes on the new Short Line railroad, and these lines offered opportunity for keen-eyed developers. By adding a depot along the way, investors could plat out new suburban towns amid the forests and farms, establishing the region's first railroad suburbs.

The most ambitious new suburb was Merriam Park, named for its banker-developer, John Merriam. By the 1890s, it was a bourgeois enclave of dozens of stately homes on the savanna between the two cities. Merriam had been a state legislator, and his son was the state's governor from 1889 to 1893, connections that led to an attempted geographic coup meant to increase the value of their land. By the 1890s, with Minnesota booming, the legislature was planning on constructing a new, larger state capitol. The Merriams lobbied to have the new capitol built next to Merriam Park, on land bordering Minneapolis along the Mississippi River (where the Town and Country golf course now sits). What's more, the Merriams' grand plan would combine the fast-growing Twin Cities, with Minneapolis and St. Paul merging into a single entity, its new capitol building at the center. Facing the prospect of such a dramatic change, interests in both Twin Cities balked, and the bill failed. The new capitol remained in St. Paul, and for a second time the city's status dodged a political bullet.

The early suburbs reflected a Victorian ethic of nature and domestic recreation, a dream built along curving streets and elaborate parks. To boost land values, the Merriams erected Union Park, a Victorian amusement grounds just north of the rail depot (near today's Fairview Green Line station). For a few years, the park was a grand nineteenth-century promenade, featuring bowling, a bandstand, a carousel, a zoo, an observation tower, and paths along which dignified couples strolled, making small talk. Pitted against the booming real estate market, the amusement park did not last long. Within years, it was scrapped in favor of the development of more upper-class homes in the fast-growing city.

A mile to the northeast sat Lake Como, one of the city's two large lakes. Years before, the lake had borne the prosaic moniker Sandy Lake, and it had a brief cameo as a "natural" health resort during the 1850s. By 1872, with the city quickly expanding, city leaders brought in famed park planner Horace Cleveland, who promptly advised them to preserve a grand park along its western shore. St. Paul floated bonds to purchase over two hundred acres adjacent to Lake Como, on the far edge of the city at the time, accessible only by a bumpy carriage ride. By the late 1880s, with the construction of the Milwaukee Road (now the Canada Pacific) line, the lake became part of the city, and a suburban development arose on the south side of the tracks.

Over the next few years, park planners transformed Como into the city's finest Victorian refuge. Acres of curving paths were paved through the oaks, while a golf course, zoo, and elaborate glass conservatory

building were built among the gardens and trees. From the very beginning, Como became a beacon of nature for the fast-growing neighborhoods on the edge of St. Paul, and today the park remains the crown
jewel of St. Paul's expansive park system.

Farther along the Northern Pacific line, at the far northwest corner of
the city, lay another suburban enclave called St. Anthony Park, another
subdivision of curving streets, small parks, and stately homes surrounding a rail station. Laid out in 1883 by the prolific Horace Cleveland, the
new suburb grew quickly, in tandem with the new agricultural campus
of the University of Minnesota. For a while, the residential settlement
retained its countryside character, but as railroad traffic boomed through
the 1890s and St. Paul kept annexing more land, the leafy enclave was
soon crowded with industry along its southern and eastern edge.

The arrival of smokestacks, grain elevators, or warehouses was a common fate for many early railroad suburbs, as rail lines typically brought

Pavilion at Lake Como, about 1907

with them lucrative industrial opportunities. By 1900, with the com-ing of the new electric streetcars, St. Paul had annexed all of the early suburbs. The contrast of curving suburban streets with smokestacks and freight trains changed the tenor of the neighborhoods. To this day, a walk along the streets to the west of St. Paul's Midway reveals an odd juxtaposition of industry and working- and upper-class homes. St. Paul's diverse character is on full display along the seams of class and opportunity.

On the other side of town, St. Paul's uneven social relationships were starkly visible in Swede Hollow, the ravine carrying Phalen Creek south between Lowertown and the bluffs east of downtown. The hollow was named for the Swedish immigrants who built secluded homes there in the 1850s. When the railroads arrived a decade or so later, the hollow formed the eastern border of "railroad island," a triangle of land sur-rounded by the city's busiest tracks. Everywhere they went, the railroads carved up the city, but nowhere as much as around Swede Hollow. For the residents, there were only a few ways in and out: crossing multiple sets of busy tracks on their way from Lowertown, climbing along the sides of the steep bluff, or walking under the Seventh Street viaduct through a unique railway tunnel, built with its masonry arranged in a helicoidal (spiral) pattern. As the area grew more industrial, the hollow became a community for people living at St. Paul's social margins, mak-ing ramshackle homes along a creek without modern amenities like plumbing. Being off the grid meant very affordable housing prices, and certain social freedoms, allowing immigrants to make their own rules, their own food, or their own wine. For a century, the hollow sheltered people who had arrived with meager savings, as they walked to and from jobs in the downtown warehouses or the East Side factories.

By far the closest employer for Swede Hollow denizens was Theo-dore Hamm's Brewing Company, a brewery founded back in 1865 along Phalen Creek. With the coming of the railroads, the brewery grew quickly, marketing natural water and its nearby caves, critical to the cold fer-mentation process. By the 1880s, Hamm's had become the city's largest brewery, and Hamm erected a massive brewery complex at the apex of

Swede Hollow. By 1887, Theodore Hamm built himself an elaborate, turreted mansion on the bluff atop the hollow, providing him an eagle's-eye view of the slapdash settlement and busy brewery.

Life was not glamorous in St. Paul's working-class enclaves, but it worked well enough. As people earned money, families moved up out of the places like the hollow or the flats into nicer homes along the thoroughfares of the fast-growing town. In this way, life turned over, and new rounds of immigrants like Italians, Poles, and Mexicans moved into the city's margins. Stark juxtapositions between rich and poor were alive everywhere in the city, around the railroad tracks and along the river, in Capitol Heights and Rondo, and in communities like Little Italy under the new High Bridge that connected the West Seventh neighborhoods with the West Side in 1888. It's easy to imagine people crossing

Swede Hollow, about 1910. A rail line cuts across the top of the rise at left; Hamm's Brewery is to the left of the smokestack; and Hamm's mansion is at top right.

the bridge and looking down at the Italian and Polish people living underfoot, gaping at those they viewed as inferior. On certain spring days, as the river rose, they may have seen families gathering their belongings into boats, paddling down the streets to the nearest dry land. Or imagine businessmen looking out from the booming downtown buildings at the immigrant community on the West Side river flats, whose residents lived in crowded hand-built apartments and bathed in the public bath house. Picture the city's Black porters and barbers, who, like many service workers of the era, maintained an uneasy relationship with the booming middle class. The gap between rich and poor was visible nearly everywhere in old St. Paul, hard to ignore.

In the midst of inequality, St. Paul's urban growth was stoked by the new interurban transit lines, beginning with the first horsecar along West Seventh Street in 1872. The horsecars ran on rickety rails on wooden beams on the often muddy streets, small trolleys drawn by weary horses at a few miles per hour. Despite the slow pace, the horsecars revolutionized travel for a walking town. The first lines connected downtown to the blossoming neighborhoods along West Seventh Street and across the new Robert Street bridge. Still, the city's uneven topography posed challenges for horses, and by the early 1880s, a cable car ran up the steep incline to Dayton's Bluff east of downtown. A steam plant powered the system to the top of the bluff, running on a moving cable underneath the street. A similar line was constructed west of town up the 12 percent grade of St. Anthony Hill along Selby Avenue, just past the Summit Avenue mansions. For years, the cable cars and horsecars worked together to provide efficient transport up and out of downtown and into the fast-growing neighborhoods on the bluffs.

The transit system took a massive leap forward when it was electrified around 1890. By then, both the Minneapolis and St. Paul transit systems were owned by Thomas Lowry, a Minneapolis lawyer who became a kingpin of regional transit and real estate. Lowry built a system around popular new interurban lines connecting Minneapolis and St. Paul via University Avenue, Como Avenue, Selby Avenue, and West Seventh Street (the latter cutting directly through the parade ground of old Fort Snelling). Electric streetcars were larger, faster, smoother, quieter, and more reliable than the old horsecars, and they quickly became the default way to travel in St. Paul. Wherever the streetcars went, homes and neighborhoods grew like seeds behind a plow. They catalyzed development along Grand, Randolph, Selby, University, Rice, Payne, Como, East and West Seventh Streets, Dale, Snelling, Robert, and a dozen more corridors besides.

In the last decades of the nineteenth century, supported by Lowry's investments and land deals, the Twin Cities streetcar system became one of the best in the country. New streets filled with shops and corner stores, and the pulse of the trolleys formed the life of the booming city. At the same time, the streetcars were synonymous with land deals. At least until the next financial crash, they proved lucrative, and many members of the Minneapolis and St. Paul elite turned to real estate development. At one point, St. Paul's ambitious Catholic archbishop, John Ireland, even joined the fray, buying interests in property around the church's new seminary on the city's west border (now the University of St. Thomas). Ireland invested heavily in land that he hoped would link to the new electric streetcar system. When the financial Panic of 1893 halted expansion, Ireland, who was named archbishop in 1888, had to be bailed out by his friend Jim Hill, who seemed to emerge stronger from every cycle of financial turmoil.

By 1905, the streetcars ran from Stillwater and White Bear Lake through St. Paul and Minneapolis far to the west. Two years later, the Selby Avenue cable car chokepoint was finally fixed by boring a tunnel in the bluff, allowing electric trolleys to climb at a gradual seven percent grade. (The sealed tunnel remains buried in the shadow of the cathedral.) A few years later, the streetcar company built a massive manufacturing facility at the corner of Snelling and University (where Allianz Field sits today). Sprawling over dozens of acres, the facility included machine shops where almost every regional streetcar was produced, maintained, and repaired in-house by hundreds of Twin City Rapid Transit workers. The St. Paul cars were so well made that some of them are still in use today in faraway San Francisco.

Just as transit helped tie the city together, St. Paulites were joiners, and the boom years were a heyday of social organizations of all stripes: societies, groups, and associations like the International Order of Odd Fellows, the Masons, the Owls, the Elks, and dozens more. There were clubs for every new nationality that made St. Paul home. The Germans had organizations like the Schubert Club, a sponsor of German classical music dating to 1893, and the Deutsches Haus, where working-class immigrants organized a flourishing labor movement. In St. Paul's African American community, centered in the neighborhood just west of downtown, Black St. Paulites formed social clubs like the Pioneer Masonic Lodge and the Sons of Freedom and literary associations like the Golden Key and the Robert Banks Society, dating back to the 1860s and 1870s. The Irish had the Society of Saint Patrick, the Ancient Order of Hibernians, and Irish Catholic parishes spread through the city. The Czechs and Slovaks erected a stately gymnastics hall in West Seventh Street's New Bohemia neighborhood, a building that hosts weddings to this day. Seemingly every sizable company sponsored a baseball team, competing in tournaments in the city's new parks and fields all over the city. At the same time, settlement houses and other improvement associations helped newcomers, in places like the Neighborhood House on the West Side or the Welcome Hall in Rondo.

The immigrants coming to St. Paul during the boom years brought with them tight religious ties, and the city filled with new churches of every denomination. Some of the oldest that remain downtown—the Church of St. Louis (1868), Assumption Catholic Church (1875), and Central Presbyterian (1889)—reflect the diverse variations of Christianity that the new immigrants brought to St. Paul. As the city boomed, the churches got bigger, and towers soon punctuated the treetops of the bustling city. The tallest was St. Agnes Catholic Church (1897), its two-hundred-foot-tall spire topped with a clock that still casts its shadow over Frogtown. The African American families who had escaped slavery and arrived via raft established Pilgrim Baptist Church, and after having two white ministers imposed by the national Baptist convention, the church welcomed Robert Hickman as its minister. Other Black churches, like St. James AME, St. Peter Claver (Catholic), and St. Mark's (Episcopal), formed the centers of social life for Black St. Paulites, connecting people with opportunity, culture, and mutual aid. Along Summit Avenue, the massive House of Hope Presbyterian Church (1909), formed from a church merger, featured the city's first carillon. In 1917, the First Lutheran Church, which was founded in 1854 by Swedish immigrants, moved from the center of town to the edge of Dayton's Bluff, following the exodus of neighborhoods from the commercial district. It still serves as a haven for unsheltered people on the edge of the East Side.

The boom years were the era of monumental construction, capped with two architectural masterpieces that still define St. Paul: the marble dome of the Minnesota State Capitol, completed in 1904, and the copper dome of the Cathedral of St. Paul, completed ten years later on Summit Avenue. Balancing the St. Paul skyline, both buildings are monuments to civic ambition heading into the twentieth century. In 1895, with the state growing rapidly and the old downtown capitol getting cramped, the legislature held a design competition for a new capitol to represent the state. The winning architect was thirty-five-year-old Cass Gilbert, who used the project to launch his national career. Construction began in 1896 at a site near the Central Park neighborhood, a community of aging mansions and townhouses on the edge of the fast-changing downtown. Gilbert's building is a stunning example of Beaux-Arts neoclassicism, constructed of white marble shipped from Georgia. In front of its innovative dome sits a statue of four golden horses called Progress of the State or, simply, the Quadriga. It depicts the twin figures of Agriculture and Industry holding bridles, while Prosperity rides in the carriage. When the building opened in 1905, it marked the beginning of the transformation for the old neighborhood along Fourteenth Street, from a dense mix of schools, industry, apartments, and aging mansions into the wide-open blocks of statues and government offices you see today.

A few years after the capitol was completed, construction began on the city's other monument, the new Cathedral of St. Paul. The church

The Minnesota State Capitol under construction, April 1902

took the site of Norman Kittson's mansion, erected in 1884 by the fur trader and Red River businessman. By then, many of the old mansions were expendable and out of date. In its place, Ireland began the construction of the cathedral that now sits on its eponymous hill. The stone facade reflects the central place of the Catholic Church in the city's politics and culture, a dynamic that proved critical to the city's political life long into the twentieth century.

The boom years saw the city's population explode, a revolution in transportation that shifted activity away from the river and onto the city's ubiquitous rails, and the platting and construction of huge swaths of the city. Many of today's middle-class neighborhoods were laid out in those years, and they are still lined with homes and shops of the diverse communities built around the old streetcar nodes. On the other hand, many of the old working-class neighborhoods are gone, especially those that were home to St. Paul's diverse ethnic groups. There's almost no trace of old Swede Hollow, as the off-the-grid community was razed in the 1950s. At the same time, many of St. Paul's largest Victorian mansions

The Cathedral of St. Paul, about 1915

met the same fate, as they were all but impossible to keep up in the cities of the twentieth century. This included the Theodore Hamm house, abandoned by the mid-twentieth century and burned by an arsonist in 1954.

Yet Summit Avenue tells a different story, and St. Paul still boasts one of the country's best-preserved mansion districts. For four and a half miles from the cathedral to the Mississippi River, almost all of the city's old mansions still stand. The James J. Hill House is now a historic site, and many of the street's ornate buildings display turrets, pillars, windows, and stones reflecting decades of changing taste. Summit remains a splendid example of America's golden age of inequality, and even now is a place for promenading, bicycling, and even an occasional croquet match.

These boom years set the tone for St. Paul's emerging identity, and you don't have to walk far along Summit Avenue to reach an astounding spot where the city inspired literature. Just east of Dale Street stands a set of red granite row homes where St. Paul's most famous writer, F. Scott Fitzgerald, lived in 1918. Growing up in St. Paul, surrounded by what one St. Paul writer called "the claws of class," Fitzgerald was living with his parents and pondering his retreat from the world of the East Coast elite. He holed up in the top floor of his parents' rented home and wrote his first great novel, *This Side of Paradise*, a tale of a young midwestern man struggling to find a place in the Ivy League.

A year later, a block away, Minnesota's first Nobel laureate lived for a while on Summit Avenue. Sinclair Lewis stayed in the Italianate home on the corner of Summit and Oakland Avenues in 1919, working on a play, before he made it big with his novel lampooning midwestern striving: *Main Street*. His career also critiqued Minnesota provincialism and the entrepreneurial boosterism so synonymous with nineteenth-century progress. It is perhaps not a coincidence that Summit Avenue became fertile ground for criticism of America's Gilded Age. That St. Paul's landscape of uneven wealth survived the twists and turns of American urban history—waves of depression, suburbanization, and neglect—is a rare feat, a testament to the city's resilience and complacency.

CHAPTER 4

Overshadowed

"Poor old St. Paul!" is one of the sneering ejaculations frequently
heard from our self-esteeming and self-satisfied friends and neighbors
in our sister city up the river. But look! "Poor old St. Paul" subscribed
$17,597,500 to the new Liberty Loan in three days, while Minneapolis,
in the same period, subscribed only $5,677,800, with all its boasted
superiority in wealth, enterprise and public spirit, and its established
superiority of nearly 100,000 population.

—*St. Paul Union Advocate*, October 19, 1917

When a New York columnist visited Minnesota in the fall of 1885, either
winter came early that year or he was in a bad mood. Either way, he
penned an infamous report about his midwestern trip, describing the
great city of St. Paul as "another Siberia, unfit for human habitation."

The quip made the rounds of barbershops and back rooms, soon becoming fodder for St. Paul's defensive boosters. The column was a direct
slap at their urban aspirations. Then, as now, Minnesota generally and
St. Paul in particular displayed heightened sensitivity to coastal slights.
While positive attention from the big cities, no matter how meaningless, was greeted with pride, negative reviews from coastal press proved
white-hot fuel for the indignant.

St. Paul's thin skin was on full display in the era when the city still
sought to be the metropolis of the Upper Midwest. "St. Paul: The Center
of North America" and similar triumphalist slogans appeared daily in
newspapers, ad pamphlets, and the annual city directory. Determined to
correct the record, St. Paul boosters—men like dry goods merchant Mau-
rice Auerbach or George Thompson, owner of the *Dispatch*—attempted
to turn the tables on the wintry condemnation, and hatched plans for a

fabulous "Winter Sports Carnival." The idea was heavily plagiarized from a similar event in Montreal, which had for years erected ice palaces in the dead of winter to attract visitors to its "healthful winter climate." Then, in the fall of 1886, Montreal experienced a smallpox epidemic. The Canadian festival was canceled, and when its ice architects were laid off, St. Paul civic leaders pounced. They brought the Canadians to Minnesota, where, forged in a fire of defensiveness and ambition, the St. Paul Winter Carnival was born.

The first carnival centered on a massive ice palace, funded by "stock" sold at ten dollars a share (the equivalent of over $250 today) to civic-minded St. Paulites. The palace contained more than twenty thousand blocks of ice cut from Lakes Phalen and Como, the St. Croix River, and elsewhere. They were hauled to Central Park, the small Victorian public space on the north edge of the city, where the palace began to rise over-looking downtown. Despite a cold snap that brought temperatures past twenty degrees below zero, over a few January weeks derricks placed the blocks ever higher among the stately mansions and row homes. When it was finally complete, the ice palace was the talk of the town. It drew crowds in the thousands from all over to wander through the fifteen-foot ice archway.

A winter king was crowned, and outdoor sports commenced with vigor. Curling, skating, tobogganing, skiing, and even a fake Native American village complete with tipis provided plenty to keep families busy during the first week of February. The castle's frozen keep was topped with a massive American flag that flapped in the cold wind, and—amazingly for 1886—electric lights were installed on the ice, making it one of the very first structures in the city to boast electricity. St. Paulites were awed by a palace lit up at night with "every color of the rainbow." To finish the festival, volunteers with torches and fireworks stormed the palace, shooting Roman candles at the ice walls and setting off fireworks. Less celebrated: once the festival was over, the palace took months to melt during the spring thaw, decaying into the kind of incongruous ice mass familiar to Minnesotans today.

The ice palace built for the winter carnival in 1888. This image was produced as half of a stereopticon view with the caption, "Royal family Equipages leaving the Winter Palace."

1565 Royal family Equipages leaving the Palace.

The winter carnival made such an impression that St. Paul boosters repeated the affair each of the next two winters, culminating in 1888 with the biggest palace yet, a grand turreted affair built from fifty thousand ice blocks, complete with an ice maze in the rear courtyard. In 1889 and 1890, however, the winters were unseasonably warm, and without a reliable supply, ice construction was canceled. All that's solid melts into spring, and the winter carnival was forgotten for a generation.

The rise and fall of the ice palaces mirrored the booster logic that dominated midwestern cities. For boosters, development was a zero-sum game. St. Paul's growth came at the expense of competitor cities—Duluth, St. Peter, Stillwater, and especially Minneapolis—and vice versa. As a result, St. Paul was locked in a valiant struggle to maintain its place as the Northwest's most important burg. These dynamics were no-holds-barred affairs, and cities throughout the region deployed advertisements, glowing publications, and vituperative public relations campaigns to attract investment, speculation, business, and immigrants.

Sadly for St. Paul's businessmen, as the nineteenth century grew to a close, the city lost economic steam. Minneapolis's industries at St. Anthony Falls, the Mississippi's valuable source of waterpower, were booming with jobs and business. Explosive economic growth was transforming Minneapolis into a magnet for both immigration and investment.

St. Paul simply could not keep up. Each year, Minneapolis's accumulating influence made it increasingly clear that St. Paul was not, after all, destined to be the next great Chicago. For city leaders, Minneapolis's new status was a difficult pill to swallow, and the business elite did not take it sitting down. Instead, they fought to maintain supremacy.

By the late 1880s, the booster battleground turned to the upcoming federal census. Population was the most obvious measure of power and influence, and the 1880 census had shown the two cities to be roughly the same size—Minneapolis actually tallied a slightly larger forty-six thousand people to the forty-one thousand in St. Paul. The upcoming 1890 census was thus fraught with political significance. If St. Paul could show that it was matching Minneapolis's growth, it would ease the anxieties of the city's business class and assuage those investing in the capital city.

State Fair

The Minnesota State Fair is older than the state itself, dating back to 1854 and the formation of the Minnesota Agricultural Society. The society's goal, like that of most newcomers in the early boom years, was to put Minnesota's bounteous resources on display and attract migrants into the territory. Fairs also helped spread best crop practices and introduced farmers to new technology. The territory's first fair took place in Minneapolis in 1855, and after statehood in 1858 the event received a promotion: the Minnesota State Fair was born.

In the early years, the fair location floated around while the society chose its grounds based on a delicate balance of political turf and settler ambition. State fairs were held in places like Owatonna, Rochester, and Red Wing, in addition to a few different locations in then-distant St. Paul and Minneapolis. By the 1870s, with the urban population booming, the fair grew beyond its agricultural roots, evolving into a more urban spectacle. As a result, rival boosters in Minneapolis and St. Paul fought over who got to play host. For five years, there were even competing fairs open simultaneously in both cities, with St. Paul hosting the "official" state fair and a Minneapolis entrepreneur named William King sponsoring his own brand of fair across the river.

Everything changed in 1885, when Ramsey County offered to donate its poor farm, a large parcel of land where the city's paupers tended fields in exchange for lodging. The farm, then located in a separate town called Hamline, was conveniently placed between the two downtowns and offered a seemingly neutral compromise. Today, the fairgrounds are technically in the suburb of Falcon Heights, but the city of St. Paul borders on three sides.

Fair traditions have evolved over the years. Butter carving began in 1898, while the llama costume contest is a more recent addition. Until the 1950s, most people arrived for the fair via the Twin City Rapid Transit streetcar system, which ran extra lines into the heart of the fairgrounds. These days, the two million people who attend the fair each year take shuttle buses from all corners of the metro or park their cars on lawns in the Como neighborhoods. For twelve nights a year, thousands leave the grounds, full of sights and food, as the nightly fireworks light up the skies of northern St. Paul.

By the time the census counts began in 1890, the battle lines were drawn, and both St. Paul and Minneapolis unleashed a chaos of statistical shenanigans. As described in a subsequent investigation, officials in both cities stretched nearly every law, adapting the time-honored motto of city machine politics: "Count early, count often." Thousands of phantom citizens of St. Paul and Minneapolis were entered into the official tally. In St. Paul, over three hundred nonexistent houses were marked on the map. Over two hundred people were listed as living in the Union Depot train station, and twenty-five in a nearby barbershop. Minneapolis did the same, listing as residents people who had been underground in cemeteries for years. Each city tried to seize the others' records, deploying sheriffs and newspaper headlines in equal rigor, and city officials released a constant stream of accusations of flimflammery. "Scheme to Swell the Population of the Flour City Knocked in the Head!" said St. Paul. "Dastardly Outrage Committed on Minneapolis Citizens by the St. Paul Gang!" said Minneapolis. The results grew so contested that the Census Bureau intervened. In Minneapolis, investigators found a widespread conspiracy that boosted results by over eighteen thousand people; in St. Paul, they uncovered small-scale fraud and incompetence that added around nine thousand. As a result, federal officials threw out the results and demanded a new census be taken, free from double-dealing and fictitious neighborhoods.

When the dust had settled, the more accurate count firmly established Minneapolis as the state's largest city: it boasted 164,000 people to St. Paul's 133,000. The wide gap meant that, from then on, St. Paulites could never again claim to be the most important city in the state. St. Paul would never again challenge Minneapolis's lead in population, wealth, economic centrality, and financial influence.

Minneapolis's industrial base gave it a different character than St. Paul's fine-grained commercial and transportation economy. The milling industry concentrated density around the downtown core and centralized power in fewer hands within the business community. In Minneapolis, jobs required larger pools of available labor, and at shift change, the city's big mills released hundreds of men on both sides of the river. The streets, bars, and commutes pulsed with the crowds. The rich men who tightly controlled the mills and factories—Minneapolis tycoons like the Washburns, the Pillsburys, and others—formed a clique that closely controlled city politics. In the meantime, the railroads and banks gave Minneapolis a near-monopoly on the northwestern grain trade, so that financiers reaped profits from the agricultural surplus of midwestern farms. Together, this Republican business class, the police force, and other city boosters forged an anti-union coalition called the Citizens

Alliance that successfully fended off the burgeoning labor movements organizing at the turn of the twentieth century.

By contrast, the key industries of St. Paul were disaggregated. The city's largest employers were the railroads, especially the Northern Pacific and the Great Northern (both partly or fully controlled by James J. Hill), as well as the Omaha Road (connecting St. Paul to Iowa). Each of the railroads employed over a thousand workers by the turn of the century, many in manufacturing and maintenance at large rail yards, on traveling crews maintaining the rails themselves, or on the well-staffed passenger lines that were the lifeblood of long-distance travel in the country. This latter group included a large number of African American porters, called Red Caps, men who staffed the passenger cars working for tips. It was one of the few reliable jobs for Black workers in St. Paul's big industries.

The rest of the city economy was more fragmented. There were big breweries that employed hundreds—Hamm's on the East Side and Schmidt's on West Seventh Street—but also smaller enterprises like Yoerg's, Brueggmann's, or North Star Brewing, and the brewery owners became social linchpins of St. Paul's business class. Meanwhile, all kinds of small manufacturing concerns were scattered around town. In 1910, one such small company, Minnesota Mining and Manufacturing, moved its failing sandpaper business from the North Shore of Lake Superior to St. Paul's East Side, where it began to turn a profit and grew quickly, eventually changing its name to 3M. Factories of all sizes scattered along the railroads running through the city, making everything from wicker doormats (Crex Carpets) to fur coats (Gordon Ferguson) to leather and canvas goods (J. W. Hulme) to steam fire engines (Waterous Company) to iron parts (St. Paul Foundry) to iceboxes (Seeger) to industrial adhesives (J. B. Fuller) to barber poles (William Marvy) and dozens of other enterprises.

Essential to a growing economy, building trades played another critical role in the city's economic landscape, creating the homes and offices popping up everywhere, a fact that would become vitally important as union organizing intensified in the young twentieth century. Wholesaling

Rail yards near Union Depot, 1918

remained another key sector in St. Paul, with merchants in Lowertown supplying goods to the region, though as the railroads continued to improve, that business slowly moved to the larger cities of Minneapolis and Chicago. St. Paul also boasted a strong publishing industry, printing all kinds of material; West Publishing, later bought by Thomson Reuters, gained a near monopoly on the publishing of legal cases that it holds to this day. Finally, the city remained a regional center for banking and insurance, as reflected by the elegant towers that formed the downtown skyline: the eight-story sandstone Germania Bank (1889), the marble foyer of the New York Life Building (1889), or the sixteen-story Merchants Bank Building (1915), covered in glazed white brick.

The people of St. Paul were a mix of European migrants and Yankee residents who had been in the city for a few generations, alongside a tight-knit African American community and a small number of Dakota and Ojibwe who made their homes in the city. Of all the groups, none made a greater impression on St. Paul's identity than the Irish. Many of the city's Irish immigrants, who spoke English and understood the legal system, began working in municipal and connected jobs like the police and fire departments, or the building trades. After all, the city's richest man had married an Irish waitress from Lowertown back in 1867; the city's Protestant elite could hardly afford to snub him. Mary Hill made sure her husband was a good friend to both the Irish community and the Catholic Church. Despite the larger numbers of the city's other groups, most people still considered St. Paul to be fundamentally an Irish town. Partly that was due to the Catholic Church, as St. Paul's archbishop, John Ireland, had helped create monumental architecture and investments—notably the cathedral, the colleges of St. Thomas and St. Catherine, the St. Paul Seminary—that inscribed Catholic culture on the St. Paul landscape. Beginning in the 1880s and 1890s with the elections of Christopher O'Brien and Frank Doran, many of the city's mayors and elected aldermen were Irish, and they played a central role in its emerging political life. Irish politicians would bequeath honorary Irish status to other St. Paulites so that Irish identity could often symbolically transcend ethnic and racial lines.

A long-standing devotion to booze remained another key dynamic that tied the town together. The city's nightlife took place in downtown taverns, bars, saloons, clubs, and brothels, a practice that left Archbishop Ireland, the city's premier moralist, at odds with his often intoxicated flock. Ireland spent years trying to persuade Catholic men to join his Father Mathew Society and commit to lives of temperance. Almost invariably, the pledge was short-lived, and attendance at the society's meetings ebbed as St. Paul's famously tempting social circles won the day and night.

All these threads came together on March 17, 1901, with the celebration of the city's largest ever St. Patrick's Day parade. The tradition dated all the way back to 1851, and as the Irish gained more prestige, the celebrations grew. In 1901, the Ancient Order of Hibernians threw an epic party to honor St. Patrick, even arranging special fares on Hill's railroad to allow people to attend. The event was a little too successful for its own good. Disavowing the "midnight orgies" that persisted through the March night, Archbishop Ireland banned future St. Patrick's Day parades in the city. The Paddy prohibition held firm until 1967, when the tradition was finally restarted at Gallivan's, a politically connected downtown Irish bar.

Archbishop Ireland and the Catholic Church were not just moderators of passions and advocates of moral virtue. They also sometimes served a mediating role within the tempestuous labor politics lurking under the surface of the Gilded Age, as left-leaning urban immigrants, farmers angry with big-city banks, and others began to organize for their rights. Through his career in St. Paul, Ireland tried to keep strikes and disputes at bay, pushing the business elite, with whom he was well connected, to make accommodation for workers, and vice versa.

St. Paul's tradition of accommodation likely began during the Great Northern strike of 1894, when James J. Hill, the city's leading businessman, came face-to-face with Eugene Debs, the founder of the Socialist Party of America. After the Panic of 1893, one of the worst economic depressions in national history, economic stagnation had gripped the city and collapsed railroads, land schemes, and businesses all through the Midwest. Ever the survivor, Hill kept his operations afloat by cutting workers' pay to forty dollars a month, hardly more than the cost of lodging. Eugene Debs, a tireless labor organizer from Indiana, was fresh off his work at the violent Pullman strike outside Chicago. He came to Minnesota trying to create a unified organization, an American Railway Union, that could transcend the fragmented worker classifications typical in the industry at the time. Instead of separate units for trackmen, engineers, mechanics, and the like, Debs wanted a single outfit to represent the thousands of Great Northern workers. When wage cuts arrived in 1894, the vast majority of the railroad's workers walked off the job on April 14.

In the midst of the financial depression, the railroad strike proved to be quite popular across the Northwest and in St. Paul. Despite his best propaganda efforts, Hill was forced to negotiate with Debs in person. On April 25, within the thick stone walls of his Great Northern building, he and Debs both proved inflexible and stubborn. Hill would not agree to broad wage increases, and Debs would not allow a compromise on his proposed union. After a nearly two-week standoff that saw most railroad traffic grind to a halt, the conflict went to arbitration, where it was decided by the Minneapolis Chamber of Commerce. Unbelievably to Hill, the arbitrators sided with the workers and imposed a compromise: Hill would raise wages and put the union men back on the job, but Debs was denied recognition for his new, larger union. The quick strike changed both men. Debs became more radicalized about American labor politics, later writing that "in all my life, I never felt so highly honored as I did when leaving St. Paul." Hill vowed never to let a strike embarrass him again. He set a tone of accommodation with labor that pervaded the thinking of most businessmen throughout the city—and held off industrial unionism.

Hill's moderate approach also sat well with St. Paul's breweries, whose leaders were some of the city's largest employers and pillars of society. At the time, the vast majority of nineteenth-century brewery workers were German-speaking immigrants, and many came to the country with liberal ideas about labor organizing. For example, the Brewer Workers

Union was explicitly Marxist, and one of the few nationwide that organized across divisions in labor, so that all types of brewery workers could
join. On top of that, since brewery workers came from the same communities as their customers, unions proved to be good business. The
brewery owners, men like Alfred Bremer, Jacob Schmidt, and Theodore
Hamm, took pains not to alienate their customer base. Keeping everyone paid well enough to buy your product was the key to success in the
beer industry.

Compared to St. Paul, Minneapolis was rabidly anti-labor. Its chamber of commerce boasted the city was the "open shop capital of America"—meaning that employees could not be required to join a union—
and unions were routinely crushed by a business and political coalition.
Nascent strikes were quelled by the Citizens Alliance, a business organization that coordinated blacklisting, funded businesses facing labor
pressure, and kept a corrupt police force of "deputies" to fight worker
militancy. St. Paul's business landscape was neither wealthy enough nor
coordinated enough to achieve any of these goals. As a result, labor disputes in St. Paul typically were small-scale and short-term, and organizers made liberal use of ostensible St. Paul communitarian values to
coerce city employers to display social responsibility. On top of that, as
the seat of government, St. Paul was the headquarters for the statewide

Schmidt Brewery, about 1905

labor movement, and a local newspaper, the *St. Paul Union Advocate,* took great pains to ensure that St. Paul employers worked with labor rather than against it. Of course, the vast majority of union workers at the time were white, and labor organizing across racial lines would not be common for many years to come.

The turn-of-the-century exception that proved the St. Paul rule occurred in 1903, when West Publishing and its president, Charles Ames, tried to form a St. Paul Citizens' Association, a version of Minneapolis's pro-business group. West executives, along with a cadre of other manufacturers and wholesalers, began lobbying for open shop rules to break labor control over the city's industries. The effort was both brief and toothless, and union organizers managed to use their ties with breweries and other well-organized shops—crate makers, suppliers, building trades, and the like—to fight Ames's group. The contest came to a head in a bombastic anti-labor speech given on November 19 by a pro-business radical named David Parry, head of the National Association of Manufacturers. It was printed the next day in the *Advocate,* and the backlash from city workers was enough to quell anti-union efforts in favor of what one historian termed "the interdependence of business and labor."

In this way, St. Paul became the Minnesota poster child for conflict avoidance. Surface-level compromise on matters of business or religion adhered closely with its civic identity as the state's second city, one that had to struggle for its share of growth and investment. To compete with neighboring Minneapolis, and its extreme levels of economic disparities and worker suppression, St. Paul tacked toward moderation. Helped by the Irish community and the Catholic Church, the city carved out a unique civic identity that managed to avoid the tumult of the early twentieth century, one that saw both strikes and industrial exploitation reach new, extreme proportions across the country.

And yet, the fissure between labor and capital occasionally crossed over the city border. The most blatant occasion occurred in 1917, when workers in St. Paul valiantly tried to organize a key Minneapolis-run enterprise, the Twin City Rapid Transit (TCRT) streetcar system. The streetcars employed thousands of folks in the Twin Cities and hundreds in St. Paul, and they were a monopoly, controlled since 1890 by Minneapolis real estate tycoon Thomas Lowry. By 1917, his son Horace was running the family business, following the default open shop anti-union practice. For the hundreds of TCRT workers in St. Paul, this did not sit well. Pressure to challenge the company had been building since Lowry had constructed a downtown St. Paul hotel, at Wabasha and Fourth Street, using nonunion labor.

In the fall of 1917, when streetcar operator wages were cut, labor activists began to organize. In response, the TCRT bosses fired over fifty union supporters while granting pay raises to the rest of the staff, a common way to divide workers. The tactic only mobilized the nascent union effort, and the resulting unrest revealed stark differences between the two cities' civics. Though TCRT workers lived in both cities, Minneapolis's pro-business Citizens Alliance hired hundreds of thugs to arrest and crack down on strikers. Meanwhile, St. Paul's elected officials did

The opening of the Grand Avenue streetcar line, February 1890

almost nothing, confident that the two sides would compromise with some kind of peaceful agreement.

They did not. When workers walked off the job on October 6, St. Paul strikers broke into a full-on riot aimed at pushing the streetcar company to cave to demands. Some workers accosted streetcar drivers who had crossed the picket line, while others began literally dismantling the streetcar infrastructure of downtown St. Paul. Men pulled down poles, tore down catenary lines, and smashed streetcar windows. St. Paul's transit system, the lifeblood of urban mobility, shut down completely. Notably, though the streetcars were damaged, the rest of downtown was almost entirely unscathed; demonstrators targeted only the Minneapolis-run monopoly. Because St. Paul's longtime police chief, John O'Connor, and the Ramsey County sheriff were both labor supporters, over the next few days they declined to adopt harsh retaliations commonplace to Minneapolis.

Striking streetcar workers in Rice Park, 1917

But soon enough, soldiers from Fort Snelling were deployed to St. Paul to stop further destruction. It turned out that 1917 was not a great year for organizing workers. The United States had joined the world war that spring, and the strike ran into political dynamics that proved poisonous to dissent in Minnesota. In order to help the war effort, Governor Joseph A. A. Burnquist, a St. Paul man himself, created a public safety commission and granted it sweeping legal powers that the group used to crack down on unrest.

Following the riot, the commission organized a settlement. They decided the dispute in favor of the streetcar company, while allowing the union members to keep their jobs. Both sides claimed victory, though in reality the workers lost. The union remained unrecognized, and the workers, including the hundreds employed at the large streetcar maintenance facility in St. Paul's Midway, did not gain a union until 1934.

The streetcar strike clarified the difference between the Twin Cities' labor cultures. Unlike Minneapolis, where the business class unified into a political machine, St. Paul, which lacked its twin's concentrations of wealth, was complex and compromised. Unions remained strong throughout the city, even if most of them operated at a small scale, and a culture of civic solidarity blunted the power of capital. Instead, St. Paul organizing culture became a spearhead for a future alliance among northern mining unions, farmers upset by monopolistic exploitation, and urban workers. It was out of this mixture that the Farmer-Labor party, and the eventual Democratic-Farmer-Labor alliance, would be crafted.

That organizing culture came into play for civic ventures as well. In 1916, after a nearly twenty-year hiatus, the St. Paul Winter Carnival returned as the "Outdoor Sports Carnival" when James J. Hill's son Louis took a personal interest in rekindling the event. Though the ice palace was only twelve feet tall, Hill himself dressed in fur and led the carnival parade through downtown St. Paul, gathering the city's leaders and workers together in the middle of winter. The carnival disappeared during the war and, despite Hill's fondness for the event, did not pop up again in the capital city until the 1930s. The carnival remained an on-and-off affair, depending on highly variable weather and financing.

It wasn't until after World War II ended that the winter carnival emerged as a celebrated annual tradition, a chance for St. Paul's civic pride to shine.

For a while, the carnival even hinted at the promise of St. Paul as a multiracial city. Beginning in 1915, an African American architect named Clarence Wigington had worked on municipal buildings, eventually rising to the title of city architect. In that position, Wigington became one of the most prominent Black architects in the country. He designed such St. Paul monuments as the Highland Park Water Tower and the pavilion on the West Side's Harriet Island. But according to one biographer, Wigington's favorite municipal role was as designer, every few years, of ice palaces for the carnival. As temporary structures, the castles allowed an architect to play with fanciful ideas and structures. Wigington must have delighted in designing and overseeing the construction for six castles from 1937 to 1947, though all traces of this work disappeared with the spring's thaw.

St. Paul's most recent palace was a perfect example of the difficulties faced by a budget-strapped city in building extravagant ice structures in an era marked by climate change. The castle coincided with the 2018 Super Bowl that placed Minneapolis, and its highly subsidized downtown stadium, at the center of the national media spotlight. As usual, St. Paul struggled valiantly to get attention, photobombing Super Bowl montages with a shining ice palace in Rice Park, the heart of St. Paul's downtown. Once again, the streets of St. Paul came alive with curling, ice sculpture, and an ice bar, all sponsored by businesses like Summit, the city's large craft brewery. St. Paul was able to take its place at the edge of the national limelight, a city weird enough to celebrate its cold winters and build temporary castles out of ice.

CHAPTER 5

Wheeling and Dealing

If they behaved themselves, I let them alone. If they didn't, I got them.
Under other administrations there were as many thieves here as when I
was chief, and they pillaged and robbed; I chose the lesser of two evils. . . .
When a man knows that I know who and where he is, and that I can put
my finger on him if I want him, he has every reason to behave himself.

—Police Chief John "The Big Fellow" O'Connor

On June 10, 1923, the *New York Times* ran an article that discussed the
massive, high-tech Ford Model T factory to be built on the Mississippi
River bluff in what is today Highland Park. For St. Paul civic boosters, it
was a glorious occasion. There was only one problem: the *Times* made
the typical East Coast mistake of ignoring St. Paul, equivocating about
the new facility's exact location and implying it would be in Minneapolis.

Arthur Nelson, the mayor of St. Paul, was highly irritated. He penned
a hasty letter castigating the Gray Lady: "As a matter of fact, the Ford
hydroelectric and manufacturing plant . . . is located entirely within the
limits of the City of St. Paul. We are doing considerable municipal adver-
tising at the present time. . . . I hope that in future articles, St. Paul may
get the recognition to which, as the home of the Ford northwest plant,
we feel it is entitled."

Nelson was incensed, not simply because of the all-too-common error.
The new Ford factory showcased St. Paul's ability to work out a crafty
deal. In nabbing the factory, St. Paul scooped its Minneapolis rival and
brokered a scheme to acquire rights (finally!) to Mississippi River waterpower to fuel industry in the city.

In this case, the prize was the new Mississippi River dam stretching
between the Twin Cities near Minnehaha Park. Engineered by the US

Army Corps of Engineers, the project aimed to increase barge traffic up the Mississippi River and provide energy at the same time. Built in 1917, it featured shipping locks alongside a high dam with a thirty-foot drop. The dam could generate eighteen kilowatts of electricity in the heart of the city, though at the time it was built there was no power plant included.

Even when under construction, nobody in the fractious Twin Cities could decide on how to use the dam's energy. Everyone wanted it: Minneapolis, St. Paul, the power company (Northern States Power), and even the University of Minnesota, which displayed a stubborn independent streak. After completion, the new dam sat mired in political impasse while frustrations mounted. At one point, St. Paul tried to sneak in a federal permit application to control the dam, citing a theoretical municipal lighting system and industrial park. The effort failed, and the water kept flowing over the dam for years, generating nothing useful for anyone.

Everything changed in 1922, when St. Paul lured Henry Ford, one of America's leading businessmen, to its then-rural riverside site. By the 1920s, Ford's Model T was a bestseller, thanks to the assembly-line manufacturing that quickly made his older factories obsolete. St. Paul business leaders enticed a well-connected industrial developer from Minneapolis named Lewis Brittin, who was familiar with Henry Ford's plans for new midwestern factories. Ford's idiosyncratic ideas about factory design fit nicely with St. Paul; for example, Ford hated "overcrowded" cities and loved places that seemed harmonious with nature. He was also obsessed with river shipping and the idea of energy independence. The site at the southwest corner of St. Paul was perfect: a bucolic, undeveloped location next to the dam, alongside railroads and the river.

The trick would be to convince bickering Minnesota interests to take St. Paul's side in the dam spat, edging out Minneapolis, the university, and the power company. In 1922, Ford launched a sweeping public relations campaign full of promises and incentives. Ford's men assured folks in northern Minnesota that they would build a railroad to Duluth to supply the factory (they didn't). They assuaged the concerns of businessmen in south Minneapolis, saying that they would help pay for a new bridge linking St. Paul and Minneapolis near the new factory (they didn't fund it). They blitzed the 1922 state fair with a showcase of Ford technology, including a large number of new Fordson tractors that they assured farmers would be on hand to get through the tough years of low crop prices (they did make some tractors at the plant, but not for long). Somehow, Ford's allies even managed to defuse concerns over the company's long-standing anti-union practices (Ford despised unions and ran an open shop). They even persuaded the labor-loving editor of the *Union Advocate*, William Mahoney, to cautiously endorse the factory plans.

City House

By the turn of the twentieth century, Minneapolis's near-monopoly on the grain trade enraged many farmers of the Upper Midwest. Minneapolis grain traders bought up grain from a vast agricultural hinterland, milled it with the power of St. Anthony Falls, and shipped it to the world. Together with the railroads, the Minneapolis Chamber of Commerce and Grain Exchange controlled shipping, storage, and prices for the entire region, forcing farmers to assume high costs for shipping and supplies and to accept low prices for their crops. As a result, turn-of-the-century politics were full of rural populism, people trying to come up with alternatives to the Minneapolis markets.

St. Paul offered one possibility, because while Minneapolis had the power of the falls, St. Paul remained the head of Mississippi River navigation. Theoretically, grain could be shipped elsewhere cheaply on barges. In 1908, a group of politically active farmers started the Equity Cooperative Exchange, an attempt to circumvent the Minneapolis traders by shipping through St. Paul.

For its part, St. Paul provided the group with free land along the Upper Levee, and the exchange built its first facility there in 1917. It could store five hundred thousand bushels of wheat, rye, oats, and barley and, theoretically, could ship it downriver to bypass the Minneapolis chamber. The only catch: river navigation remained undependable. The Mississippi was unpredictable, and the river depth varied widely depending on the season. The exchange failed, and the Minnesota Farmers Union took over the facilities. By 1930, following a new federal policy that built dozens of new locks and dams and dredged the Mississippi to its current nine-foot depth, the effort expanded. The reorganized Minnesota Farmers Union erected a complex of over sixty silos, a mill, and a sack-loading facility near the old Upper Landing. By 1940, the St. Paul Municipal Elevator and Sackhouse was shipping seventeen million bushels of grain downriver to market, providing farmers with a cooperative competitor to the Minneapolis Grain Exchange.

The downtown complex was finally decommissioned in the 1980s and replaced with a nearby elevator, still in operation further upstream. Part of the mothballed complex remained at the edge of downtown for years before finally being restored and remodeled in 2016 into a seasonal café and event space. During the warm months of the river navigation season, visitors to the riverfront can stop at the old elevator on Mill Street, rechristened the City House, and enjoy a snack or a drink. It's the best place to watch tugboats from the nearby Upper River Services park barges on the river piers, and St. Paul's working Mississippi shipping hub remains on full display.

With Ford's support, the Twin Cities dam standoff broke St. Paul's way. Tempted by the prospect of the factory, even Minneapolis business leaders broke ranks with their handpicked mayor, George Leach, who tried in vain to claim the dam for municipal electricity. By the summer of 1923, having secured the electrification rights, Henry and Edsel Ford were on-site in St. Paul surveying their domain. They soon built a neoclassical 130-acre car factory that stretched along the river bluffs and spurred a huge amount of residential development in the St. Paul hinterlands. The city pitched in funds for new roads, a new bridge, and extended streetcar lines in the new Highland neighborhood. Massive parks and golf courses were laid out on the high ground just to the east, and a new round of real estate fever swept St. Paul. By 1926, the new factory was employing thousands of men, though all but one were white. Over the next few years, the factory drew on the Mississippi River power and the latest in industrial technology to make Model Ts and Model As for thousands of new Minnesota drivers.

While Highland was booming, 1920s economic growth came with a catch for many in St. Paul. The 1919 passage of the Eighteenth Amendment, banning sale or transport of alcohol, eviscerated beer brewing, one of the city's main industries. This hit St. Paul's large German American community hard, as did the crackdown during the war against so-called "dissidents." Between 1917 and 1919, the Minnesota Commission of Public Safety used the fig leaves of loyalty and patriotism to silence the nascent left-wing political movements and shut down German-language schools and newspapers, many of which were based in St. Paul. Most

The Ford Motor Vehicle Plant, as seen from the Minneapolis side of the Mississippi River in 1938. The lock is in the foreground; the new dam is at left, with the white hydroelectric plant next to it; the building with the smokestack is the steam plant, which produced additional power.

Interior of the Ford plant, under construction, about 1924

troubling, the editor of St. Paul's German-language *Volkszeitung* newspaper, Frederick Bergmeier, was thrown in jail for the entire war, in a violation of basic civil rights.

Meanwhile, for much of the city, Prohibition did not sit well in practice. From its inception as Pig's Eye, St. Paul maintained a proud and consistent tradition of flouting liquor restrictions, and many saloonkeepers were well versed in evading the bans on Sunday booze. So as Prohibition arrived in 1919, St. Paul was poised to become the regional center for bootlegging. Minnesota's long, sparsely populated Canadian border and St. Paul's thick network of railroads made the city a providential location for smugglers. While most of the city's breweries switched to making weak "near beer," some breweries somehow kept brewing the full-strength stuff, which was also smuggled to preferred customers throughout the city.

In this way, Prohibition and bootlegging fit neatly within the already wink-and-nod culture of St. Paul, where, as one story put it, breweries had long used booze for political leverage. One St. Paulite, a Jewish denizen of the West Side Flats, remembered the era: "My father was the political king of the Flats, of the Shtetl. [Police Chief] Boss O'Connor ran the city. All Democrats. The breweries were big factors in politics. So a few weeks before an election, our basement mysteriously would be filled with beer to persuade the voters."

It wasn't just beer. St. Paul during the 1920s was chock-full of moonshine and other home-distilled liquors—the best was a corn liquor from Stearns County called Minnesota 13. As Prohibition forced the city's saloons and gambling dens into the underworld, all sorts got in on the action, from cab drivers to barbers to bellhops to cops. For example, some of the city's African American porters, men who worked as assistants on long-distance passenger trains, profited from Prohibition. Melvin Carter Jr., who grew up in the Rondo neighborhood, remembered that it was common to make some extra money while working as a Red Cap porter during the Prohibition era: "The Empire Builder ran from Chicago through St. Paul to Seattle [where porters had access to Canadian booze]. Fellas stockpiled boxes of whiskey. . . . On the return trip, at some prearranged clandestine location in North Dakota, the train slowed to about five miles per hour. Crates of whiskey were then tossed off the car to someone waiting for them."

Prohibition tied together the old-school city machine built around policing and vice. One of the city's most famous residents was a madam named Nina Clifford, who ran a brothel just down the bluff from downtown's high-brow Minnesota Club, where city bigwigs would sink into large leather chairs in rooms full of cigar smoke. The relationship between the elite and the underworld was an open secret in 1920s St. Paul, where judges, madams, and bootleggers occupied the same small circles.

Longtime police chief John Joseph O'Connor's early history neatly parallels the story of St. Paul. O'Connor arrived in St. Paul in 1857 as an infant. His father, "Honest John" O'Connor, an Irish immigrant who moved the family from Kentucky, worked as a grocer and made fast friends in St. Paul's growing Irish community. He was soon elected to the state legislature, and his connections helped get his son into the increasingly Irish ranks of the St. Paul Police Department. The younger O'Connor made detective in 1881 and was appointed police chief by 1900.

John O'Connor was a legendary figure. While he was in office, many people in the city were amazed at his almost preternatural ability to

Police Chief
John J. O'Connor, 1912

know exactly where to find criminals, while others realized the gift came hand in hand with what was known as the O'Connor system. While O'Connor was chief, and for over ten years after he retired, criminals in St. Paul were required to follow three basic rules. Within a day of arriving in town, they checked in with O'Connor's point men at the Green Lantern Saloon, a hole-in-the-wall joint on the north edge of downtown, and told them where they were staying. Second, they kicked back bribes to the cops, who paid people off to look the other way. And finally, they had to promise not to commit crimes within city limits. In exchange, criminals had free rein to roam St. Paul unmolested, and would be sure to get tipped off by the police about possible raids or impending arrests.

Criminals in on the deal would inform on their colleagues for stepping out of line, and O'Connor took pleasure in personally administering the beatings they would receive when they were caught. Mug shots would splash on the front pages of the next day's paper, or the cops would make a big show of demolishing slot machines or busting up a den of thieves that had broken the rules. Despite the attention, most of the time it was little more than a big show, O'Connor's boys performing for their audiences on both sides of the law.

The O'Connor system proved lucrative for folks in the vice business, anyone running one of St. Paul's famous nightclubs, gambling joints, brothels, or pool halls. Gangsters and crooks partied as you'd expect, and for years afterward, waiters at downtown sandwich shops swapped stories about fat tips they earned from people like John Dillinger or Homer Van Meter. If you were a criminal, the system was similarly slick. Crooks appreciated having an oasis amidst the fragmented justice systems that stretched across Minnesota in the early twentieth century.

The main victims of the scheme, on the other hand, were those unlucky enough to be living in nearby cities. St. Paul became a home base for crooks to run crime sprees throughout Minnesota and the Midwest. As Prohibition took hold, and liquor running became the default underworld pastime, bootlegging, gambling, money laundering, heists, and violence grew at alarming rates.

The city's gangster epicenter was the Green Lantern, a narrow, dingy joint, halfway down an alley, that featured booths on one side and a long bar on the other. If you walked in, you could be sure that both the bartender and the waitress were sizing you up, and that at least one of them was packing. The Green Lantern was where the tip-offs were made, bribes were exchanged, and schemes were hatched, either in booths or in the back corner crammed with crooks, pickpockets, and hoods. The bar's various owners worked with O'Connor and the cops by taking calls on the pay phone. In the beginning, it was a man named Reddy Griffin; after he died of apoplexy, Dapper Danny Hogan took over in 1913 and kept the system alive.

On the other extreme of St. Paul's gangster era lay the city's famous clubs and speakeasies. On University Avenue sat the Boulevards of Paris, a spacious dance club where bigwigs, crooks, and politicians alike enjoyed music and spent an intemperate night out. Across the river, embedded in the West Side bluffs, you could find the Mystic Caverns and the Castle Royale. Both nightclubs had been carved from sandstone caves that went far back underground, often featuring side exits for quick departures if the need should arise. Far to the west, on East River Road, the Hollyhocks Club awaited those with refined palates. Run by Jack Peifer, a former carnival barker, the club and casino were legendary during the Prohibition years for both the highest and lowest members of society. The first floor was a restaurant, but the second floor offered a gambling den full of craps tables, roulette wheels, and card games. The booze flowed freely, and assorted grifters and hotshots could blow off steam.

Most St. Paul bootlegging was overseen and condoned by the unofficial liquor boss, Benny Gleeman. Along with counterparts over in Minneapolis, Gleeman and his buddies created a power-sharing arrangement where each respected the others' turf. Gleeman was convicted of murder in 1925, and a new bootleg boss got out of the joint the very next year. Leon Gleckman, aka the Al Capone of St. Paul, had been doing time in Leavenworth for liquor conspiracy. The son of Russian immigrants from Minsk, he was equally adept at bribery and bootlegging. In a short time, he ran the city's criminal enterprises from the third floor of the St. Paul Hotel, arranging imports, distribution, and protection, and making money off the streams of booze running through the city.

If you overlooked corruption, O'Connor's St. Paul worked well, and everyone made money. But that all changed overnight after the crash of October 1929, which plunged St. Paul back into financial panic and economic depression. In his memoir, the African American photographer Gordon Parks described how the shadow of the Great Depression swept over the lives of nearly everyone in the city. Parks had moved to St. Paul from rural Kansas as a teenager, and he had spent years living precariously while attending high school. By 1929, he was working as an attendant at the Minnesota Club, lighting the cigars of civic notables such as former senator Frank Kellogg and Supreme Court Justice Pierce Butler.

"I couldn't imagine such financial disaster touching my small world," Parks wrote. "It surely concerned only the rich. . . . By mid-December, Hoover's promises were meaningless and hard times had settled in. My kinfolk had, like many others, lost their jobs and their credit. They were just hanging on."

St. Paul's only silver lining was that, along with Ramsey County, the city had floated $4 million in bonds the year before to fund construction of a new city hall and county courthouse. The building was planned for the heart of St. Paul next to the Wabasha Bridge, where it would symbolize the city's place in the urban pantheon. By the time construction began in 1931, the costs for everything from labor to land to materials had plunged. As a result, architects and designers had a lavish budget that stretched much further than planned. The eighteen-story building spared few expenses, and remains an art deco masterpiece, overflowing with detail, artwork, and material flourishes. The walls are made from limestone shipped from Indiana; each floor features lavish wood paneling from a distinct species of tree from around the world (for example, Brazilian rosewood on the twelfth floor and Hawaiian Koa on the sixth). The high-ceilinged atrium was built from black marble under a gold-leaf ceiling, the elevator doors from bronze, and light fixtures from brass. To this day, the elaborate deco clocks and scores of other flourishes make a trip down the hallway a treat for the eyes.

St. Paul City Hall and Ramsey County Courthouse interior, 1938

The building's grandest feature was a sixty-ton, thirty-eight-foot-tall onyx statue of a Native American man holding a peace pipe that dominates the lobby. The statue, carved by the pacifist Swedish sculptor Carl Milles, was inspired by a ceremony he once saw in Oklahoma. Originally titled *Indian God of Peace*, the statue was dedicated to World War I veterans. (It was later renamed *Vision of Peace*, to try to become less culturally appropriative.) Visitors walking the corridors near the city council chamber can regularly catch a glimpse of the giant onyx head of a mythical Native American man staring back at them between the brass louvers of the massive foyer.

As the Depression played out in St. Paul, it was not the new courthouse that took a starring role in the upcoming drama. That honor went instead to the old federal courthouse, which served many duties over the years as a post office and customhouse. With its clock tower overlooking Rice Park, the 1892 Romanesque building (now renamed the Landmark Center) was where the city's most notorious gangster trials took place.

The trials marked the unraveling of the long-lived O'Connor system. The deprivations of the Depression, combined with the end of Prohibition in 1933, put extra pressure on the uneasy relationship between St. Paul's government, police, and underworld. Back in 1928, the boss of the Green Lantern and the O'Connor system's conduit, Dapper Dan Hogan, had been killed by a car bomb while starting his Paige coupe. The crime went unsolved, and although before he expired in the hospital Hogan proclaimed "I didn't know I had an enemy in the world," most in the St. Paul underworld suspected his deputy, Harry Sawyer. Sawyer was now in charge of funneling the crooks into and out of the city and passing bribes and info back and forth to the police.

Hogan's explosive demise marked the beginning of the end of St. Paul's O'Connor arrangement. The new chief, "Big Tom" Brown, an O'Connor protégé who had risen to power as head of the "purity squad," also had close contacts with the city's criminals. By 1930, with help from political benefactors, Brown had taken over and would become one of the most corrupt leaders the city had ever seen. But calls for reforms to city government were growing louder, coming particularly from the left. In 1932, longtime St. Paul labor advocate William Mahoney ran a mayoral campaign on a reformist law-and-order Farmer-Labor ticket and won. He installed a less accommodating police chief who made an unfortunate error while cracking down on crime: he arrested two gunmen with ties to St. Paul's notorious Barker-Karpis gang who had been hiding out for years under police protection. Though both suspects posted bail and skipped town, the arrest broke the long-standing O'Connor truce. With the agreement seemingly called off, the Barker-Karpis gang went on a spree.

By then, St. Paul was a hub for bank robbers terrorizing the Midwest. People like Indiana's John Dillinger and Kansas's Alvin "Creepy" Karpis used the city as a base of operations. As Karpis described it, he was getting revenge on the bankers he blamed for the crash of '29. So many robbers lived in St. Paul that, by 1932, a full 21 percent of the nation's bank holdups took place in Minnesota. (Minnesota only had two percent of the US population.)

Few St. Paul thugs were more violent than the Barker-Karpis gang. Aside from Karpis, there were the Barker boys, Fred and Doc (née Arthur), who lived for years in and around St. Paul using their mother, Ma Barker, as cover. After the police chief's arrests broke the truce, the Barker-Karpis gang took the next step. Fresh from robberies in Wahpeton, North Dakota; Redwood Falls; and Cambridge, the gang aimed closer to home and held up the Third Northwestern Bank on the corner of Hennepin and Central Avenues in Northeast Minneapolis. The robbery took place in full view of Nordeast residents, some of whom watched through the bank's large plate glass windows.

But the robbery quickly turned into a shootout when nearby police arrived. Gangster Lawrence "the Chopper" DeVol opened up his machine gun on the approaching police car, killing both officers, but not before a stray bullet hit the gang's getaway vehicle, a Lincoln carrying the crew and their $120,000 in loot.

They drove the Lincoln to St. Paul's Como Park, where they had stashed another car. Full of adrenaline, they were in the midst of transferring the money from one trunk to the other when a pair of unsuspecting St. Paulites drove by in their Chevrolet. The two friends had been selling Christmas wreaths door to door, and, when they slowed down, a young man named Oscar Erikson craned through the window to look at the scene. As a gang member described it, Fred Barker "lost his topper and started to fire." As the bank robbers made their getaway, Erikson died the next morning.

The Como Park killing made headlines. For the first time in a long time, the O'Connor system broke down and innocent people in St. Paul paid the price. But rather than retreat into obscurity, the Barker-Karpis gang decided to not just bend but break the St. Paul rules. They would smash them into smithereens, launching a kidnapping spree that targeted St. Paul's social elite.

The first victim was none other than the president of the city's largest brewery. William Hamm Jr. was grandson of brewery scion Theodore Hamm, who had started the operation back in 1865. By 1933, William Hamm was forty years old and made his home on Dayton's Bluff, next to the brewery that bore his name. The gang hired a kidnapping expert from Chicago to plan the job, and even paid former police chief Tom Brown (who still worked in the department) to tip them off about heat from investigators. On June 15, Hamm was pushed into the back of a car, blindfolded, and driven across Wisconsin to a small Chicago suburb. The gang kept him holed up for four days while his family gathered $100,000 in ransom. By this time, St. Paul breweries had seen good profits again after years of Prohibition, and the brewery used an underworld connection to deliver the payment. Hamm was shaken up but unharmed, and his release was a sensational story that played out each day on the front pages of dozens of newspapers.

The kidnapping led to a quick change of tactics for police in St. Paul. By then, J. Edgar Hoover's FBI was on the scene working kidnapping and bank robbery cases. Most importantly, Hoover's men could do an end run around the St. Paul Police Department, deploying wiretaps and well-funded investigators to track down the elusive kidnappers. The federal help proved useful when, six months later, the Barker-Karpis gang

Reporters and onlookers at the Hamm residence after the kidnapping of William Hamm Jr., 1933

struck again. This time, they kidnapped Edward Bremer, the president of St. Paul's Commercial State Bank and son of Adolph Bremer, the owner of the Schmidt Brewery. On January 17, 1934, they boxed in Bremer's Lincoln while he was on his way to work after dropping his kids off at school. Bremer was bludgeoned before he was blindfolded and driven back to the gang's hideout near Chicago.

This time, thanks to the feds, it didn't work out so well for the gang. They got their money and Bremer was released, but the federal investigation made clear what was going on behind the scenes. The telephone at the Green Lantern was wiretapped, and the regular calls from cops tipping off crooks exposed the system for all to see. The next year, the pressure grew, and both Barker boys and even Alvin "Creepy" Karpis had been nabbed. It was during this time that America's most notorious bank robber, John Dillinger, made a stay in St. Paul, blasting his way out of a

Lexington Parkway apartment building during a police raid. The shoot-out did not add credibility to St. Paul's purported culture of public safety.

After Karpis was captured in Louisiana, he was flown back to St. Paul for a high-profile trial in the old federal courthouse. He was convicted and sent to Alcatraz, and within a year half the St. Paul police force had quit or been forced to resign. The O'Connor system was all but dead, and city officials promised to clean up corruption for good.

Though the Depression lasted a few more years, the events of the 1930s marked a shift in how St. Paul business was done. The streets of the old city were lined with saloons and home to a thriving nineteenth-century political machine. In the early days, the brothels and blind eyes of the law had their heyday. But a different city, full of proper unions and legitimate business, was struggling to take center stage. Enterprises like the shiny new Ford plant in Highland Park and the rekindled breweries

Alvin Karpis in handcuffs, entering the Federal Courts Building on Rice Park, 1936

were leading St. Paul out of the Depression, while the New Deal's Works
Progress Administration and Civilian Conservation Corps began to put
men back to work and bring artists into the city to chronicle the struggles
of daily life.

The new St. Paul City Hall and Ramsey County Courthouse was not
the only big change to downtown. City officials seized the opportunity in
1932 to undertake St. Paul's first large urban renewal project. For eighty
years, old Third Street had been St. Paul's main drag. It ran along the
bluffs over the riverfront and was lined with shops, saloons, and every
type of nineteenth-century commercial enterprise. In 1932, it was demolished in a grand gesture. In its place, the city built a large bluff-side park,

The 1931 First National Bank building on Fourth Street, a downtown art
deco icon, performs a fundamental service to St. Paul's civic identity. Its
fifty-foot "1st" sign blinks red each night. While the bank no longer exists, the
message—"We are #1"—remains a persistent declaration of civic importance
in the face of Minneapolitan dominance.

replete with fountains and wide rows of City Beautiful–style trees, along-side a wide boulevard named after former US senator and famous St. Paulite Frank Kellogg. The new road also featured ample parking for the St. Paul–built Fords clogging the downtown, and allowed the stately new 1930s buildings—city hall, the old federal courthouse, and the First National Bank, with its bright red "1st" neon sign—to be appreciated properly, without older brick structures in the foreground.

To commemorate the event, a new city flag was designed, boasting a crest that featured Galtier's cabin, the capitol dome, and a car wheel with wings to celebrate a new transportation era. When the flag was presented to the city leaders by the chamber of commerce, it ushered in a vision of a modern St. Paul that would leave the worst of the past behind. At least, that was the story.

CHAPTER 6

Bulldozer

Did you ever watch a house that you loved die in the name of progress, to make way for a parking lot? Away back in 1884 my dear Irish grandfather, who'd arrived with his bride just before the coming of Minnesota's statehood, built his third and final home, on Capitol Hill just across Cedar Street from the east door of the capitol. A few weeks ago I watched a while as the clam bit into it. . . . This sturdy old house, sliced from roof to cellar like a giant three-layer cake. . . . Another house is razed in the Capitol Approach area, this time to make room for state parking.

—Letter written to a *Pioneer Press* columnist, 1958

In 1950 St. Paul, if you stood on the steps of the cathedral looking down on the town below, you would have seen a dense and varied city stretching out block after block to the Mississippi River. Twenty-five years later, the view would be almost unrecognizable, as the years following World War II found St. Paul poised for change.

Between the cathedral, the state capitol, and downtown lay one of the city's oldest working-class areas, a maze of streets coming together willy-nilly. Factories, apartment buildings, old Victorian mansions, hovels, bars, recreational clubs, and corner shops were all mashed together and full of people. Just to the south, the Seven Corners neighborhood lived up to its name, a collision of narrow, busy streets and streetcar tracks forming St. Paul's liveliest jumble, surrounded by aging buildings caked in crumbling detail.

Downtown crowds were thicker than anything this side of the state fair, attracted by a city full of department stores displaying all the latest things. Downtown was the shopping center for the whole eastern half

Downtown St. Paul from the top of the cathedral, 1950

The state capitol from the top of the cathedral, 1950

of the Twin Cities, the place for errands and work and where all the streetcar lines crossed.

The result was a logjam of people, goods, and vehicles. As one newspaper columnist described the sight: "Close up, the city is lines of cars, darting in and out of threading traffic; it is the people who pour out of the buildings at noonday, who form a glut of humanity at Seventh and Wabasha, who jostled each other amid a rustle of packages on the buses that weave out of the Loop at 5 P.M."

But little of the old city would last much longer, as different patterns of urban development would be trumped by plans and progress. The old walking city, with its diverse chaotic neighborhoods on the edge of downtown, was targeted for removal. So too were the streetcars—on their last financial legs, slated to be replaced with buses and the speed of the motor era. The new St. Paul, driven by huge postwar federal investments, would feel radically different from the old, leaving only pockets of the older city landscape behind.

The city's urban patchwork hid a deeper truth about American cities. Vague concerns over immigration and thinly veiled racism intensified during the labor shortages of the early twentieth century, which saw increasing numbers of immigrants from places like Mexico and southern and eastern Europe. In addition, by the early twentieth century, the Great Migration of Black Americans coming north from southern states

Charles Schulz

Walk around St. Paul with a keen eye, and pay particular attention to entrances of shops or park benches. You'll start to see them: *Peanuts* characters scattered around the city like kids playing hide-and-seek. Lucy, Charlie Brown, Snoopy, Linus, and the others stand next to doorways or alongside benches, silently doing their thing. St. Paul is the perfect place for the *Peanuts* kids, because their creator, Charles Schulz, based a lot of his famous strips on his childhood in the city.

Like F. Scott Fitzgerald before him, Schulz made key creative breakthroughs as a young man while living with his parents in a St. Paul apartment. His father, Carl, worked for forty-five years cutting hair at a barbershop at the corner of Snelling and Selby Avenues. Running a three-stool hole-in-the-wall, Carl Schulz worked six days a week. On his off day, he treasured reading the Sunday comics. Charles, known as Sparky, was born in 1922 and grew up as an only child in a house on Macalester Street with his parents.

Apart from a year spent in Northern California and three years in the army during World War II, Schulz spent his formative years in St. Paul. A precocious kid a year younger than his classmates, Sparky attended St. Paul Central High School. He spent most of the school years in the background of events, developing a love of sports and forming the memories he would later mine for the rest of his career.

Schulz began drawing as a boy, and he enrolled shortly before high school graduation in a Minneapolis correspondence art school then popularly known as the Draw Me! School (now Art Instruction Schools). After his mother died, Schulz and his father moved into a small apartment above the barbershop, from which Schulz regularly mailed drawings to the school. He brought his sketchbook with him when he was drafted to serve in World War II, drawing scenes from the front, and he got good enough that he became an instructor at the school when he returned. Along the way, he developed his first distinctive one-panel strips.

Schulz inherited his father's workaholic nature and tirelessly honed his craft, drawing religious strips for a Roman Catholic comic magazine and later selling a one-panel strip named *L'il Folks* to the *St. Paul Pioneer Press*. A tireless promoter, Sparky regularly took the train from the Union Depot to Chicago and New York to pitch strips to the big newspaper syndicates. In 1950, one of the train trips paid off, and Schulz sold his four-panel cartoon, now renamed *Peanuts*.

Soon, *Peanuts* and its round-headed crew of kids became a huge hit, especially the anxious Charlie Brown and his dog, Snoopy. Schulz bought a fancy new house in Minneapolis, and eventually moved to California, though his *Peanuts* always retained its humble St. Paul sensibilities. The old barbershop became part of O'Gara's, an Irish bar, before being torn down in 2018. A new apartment building now occupies the site.

had begun. St. Paul's Black community grew steadily, increasing racial anxieties for white residents raised on intolerance.

Beginning around World War I, many of St. Paul's residential developments began to include special covenants in their mortgages, restricting future sales of homes to anyone who was not white and Christian. These racial covenants reinforced the class stratification and ethnic segregation that formed the de facto borders of St. Paul's distinct residential neighborhoods.

Living with de facto racial segregation was an everyday experience for St. Paul's communities of color, including the small Native American, Mexican American, and Asian American populations, but especially for the city's tight-knit Black community. The vast majority of Black St. Paulites lived in only a few neighborhoods, areas just on the edge of downtown and stretching to the east from the capitol and cathedral. To move outside of these segregated confines was to challenge the unwritten rules of St. Paul's white society. It was rarely attempted, and with good reason.

The unspoken truth of St. Paul segregation burst into the open in 1924, when a Black lawyer and his activist wife, William and Nellie Francis, bought a house in the middle-class Macalester-Groveland neighborhood. Nellie Francis had spent years advocating for the rights of both African Americans and women, including lobbying the legislature to pass anti-lynching laws. William Francis was earning good money working for the railroads, and the couple saw no reason why they shouldn't live in one of St. Paul's nicer neighborhoods. They bought a modest house on Sargent Avenue, but when their neighbors realized what was happening, the community erupted in a fit of organized racism.

The Francises lasted in the home for less than three years. Bigoted neighbors quickly formed a neighborhood "improvement association" and tried to buy them out. After they refused, the deluge of harassment began: marches in front of the Francis home, threatening phone calls, and, twice, burning crosses in their yard. The Francises had to hire a security guard to keep the racist mob at bay, and the standoff ended only when William Francis was appointed to a foreign service position in Liberia. Their horrid tale is one of many similar stories of the racial lines undergirding the city, stories that rarely made it into the historical record.

Inspired by early urban planning and sociology, with the hope of enacting homeownership policies that would boost the economy, New Deal inspectors began studying urban neighborhoods across the country in 1932. Unfortunately, the Home Owners' Loan Corporation (HOLC) inspectors harbored biases that lay the foundation for generations of racial inequality in America. Ostensibly grading which neighborhoods were good investments worthy of federal insurance, they baked into their assumptions racist prejudice about age, diversity, and heterogeneity of communities. All-white, single-family residential areas were given an A or B rating, while older, mixed-use, or racially diverse areas were marked with a D and colored red. These redlined parts of town—including most of St. Paul's diverse, working-class neighborhoods—became ineligible for federal insurance. Overnight it became almost impossible to sell or buy a house if you were not white.

These New Deal maps mirrored the city planning values that guided St. Paul's postwar transformation, visions of an ideal city that stemmed from the poverty of the Great Depression. At the time, urban reformers had deep concerns about urban poverty and pathologized dense neighborhoods of fast-growing cities like New York, Chicago, and (even) St. Paul. Most believed that crowded apartments, intergenerational communities, and multiethnic neighborhoods led to immorality, vice, and crime, assumptions stemming from prejudice about immigration and race.

By this logic, St. Paul needed to reform its older, heterogenous neighborhoods in favor of the kind of civic order, separation of home and work, and racial homogeneity that planners believed was the foundation for public health and moral living. Early plans were explicit about these goals; as one analysis put it, "[St. Paul] should be made as attractive as possible—by tried and tested means—to investors and to middle- and upper-class residents: and the city has some responsibility to serve the needs of its own low-income residents, but it should not make itself

attractive to a flood of low-income migrants." In the early 1950s, the
only political controversy was whether St. Paul should pay attention to
the needs of its working-class communities at all.

It was in this postwar moment that St. Paul leaders, with support
from state legislators, seized on opportunities provided by new federal
funding. St. Paul became the first city in the country to apply for public
housing aid under the 1949 National Housing Act, and the planners'
first target was the old neighborhood around the State Capitol. As
described in the federal HOLC report, it was the community most in
need of housing investment: "The district . . . is very hilly and inacces-
sible. Property values are very poor. Very heavy racial encroachment

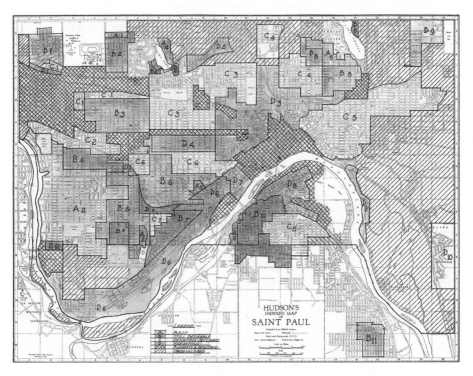

In the 1930s, the Home Owners' Loan Corporation (HOLC) coded the
neighborhoods on a street map of St. Paul: A, green, "Best"; B, blue, "Still
Desirable"; C, yellow, "Definitely Declining"; D, red, "Hazardous." Business
and industrial areas are covered with cross-hatching, and undeveloped areas
are marked with slanted lines.

throughout the entire district is prominent. The only redeeming feature is its accessibility to the downtown district."

With a fast-growing state government, legislative leaders also wanted more office buildings and parking lots for new office workers. The solution was to remake the state capitol area around architect Cass Gilbert's 1904 City Beautiful vision, which called for long avenues similar to those in Washington, DC. In practice, the plans meant demolishing nearly every block of the old neighborhood between Capitol Heights and downtown, and led by the city's Housing and Redevelopment Authority, this is exactly what happened. Throughout the late 1950s, the streets around the capitol were condemned and cleared, replaced by much wider roads, grassy open space, parking lots, and office buildings.

Most residents saw Capitol Approach renewal as a big win for St. Paul, the replacement of the unsightly older neighborhoods with a modern city, including St. Paul's first big-box store, a midcentury modern Sears. As one *New York Times* report described the new urban landscape: "Long dominated by Minneapolis, St. Paul suddenly blossoms forth with a spectacular redevelopment program. It cleared acres of slums and exposed the State Capitol in its full beauty in a parklike setting. 'We finally realized,' said one Minneapolis businessman, 'that the good grey lady across the Mississippi River has kicked off her high button shoes, put on saddles and was beginning to run like hell.'"

Not everyone was as jubilant about the changes. One *Pioneer Press* columnist took an elegiac tone as he reported on the displaced people and demolished homes: "There isn't much left of the old Thirteenth Street neighborhood, below the capitol, except some grown-over foundations. The houses are all gone and the street is a tree-lined wilderness in the twilight between the past and urban renewal."

The Capitol Approach set the tone for St. Paul's short-term future. In 1959 alone, over 2,400 homes were torn down in the name of urban renewal, wider streets, and the freeway program. Only half as many new public housing units were built to replace what was lost. Acres of city land lay empty. The aging homes were gone, while other institutions—the Deutsches Haus, a civic center for the city's historic German American community; the Mechanic Arts High School, one of the two high schools for youth from the Rondo neighborhood; and the Merriam Mansion, which housed the Science Museum of Minnesota—lingered on for years.

In the same way, postwar bulldozers cleared all traces of the flood-prone Little Italy community underneath the Smith Avenue High Bridge. When they lost their homes, many of the Italian and Polish families simply moved up the bluff to higher ground and began again along West Seventh Street. A similar fate awaited Swede Hollow, which by the 1950s had increasingly become a haven for Mexican immigrants seeking affordable housing. Like the vast majority of people of color during the urban renewal period, thanks to the racism ingrained in the landscape, they had far more difficulty than their white neighbors in finding other places to live.

At the time, most of St. Paul's Mexican Americans had lived for decades on the West Side, across the river from downtown. By the 1950s, it was the largest and most stable Mexican community in the state. Mexicans on the West Side traced their roots back to the labor shortages of World War I, when the sugar beet farmers in the Red River Valley brought Mexican migrants north to work the fields. When the harsh prairie winters arrived, given the uninsulated company housing, Mexican workers and their families needed somewhere else to go. Instead of returning to Texas, many chose the convenience of living in St. Paul. Over the years, the West Side evolved into a Midwest barrio norteño, with hundreds of Mexicans finding homes in the diverse working-class community on the flats.

The West Side neighborhood was a likewise diverse working-class enclave along Wabasha, Robert, State, and Concord Streets. But most of its housing needed maintenance, and the 1930s HOLC reports described the area in harsh, racial terms: "a ghetto district—Russians, Jews, Mexicans, Chinese, and riff-raff live here, the most undesirable district in Saint Paul." But to hear people who lived there describe it, the flats were a thriving community rich with social connection. Many of the immigrants who came to St. Paul worked in the Armour and Swift meatpacking plants a few miles down Concord Avenue in South St. Paul.

Both facilities employed thousands of workers in the slaughterhouses, butchering hogs and cattle in one of the country's largest meatpacking facilities.

The West Side boasted a mix of grocers, shops, pool halls, industry, and bars. Mexican American kids like Augie Garcia, who grew up on the flats, lived and thrived in the new barrio, and Garcia would go on to be one of St. Paul's early rock 'n' roll icons, penning a big jump blues hit with his song "Hi Yo Silver" in 1955. Often lacking infrastructure commonplace in wealthier parts of St. Paul, people on the flats made do. In those years, Harriet Island, still surrounded by water, connected to the flats by a long wooden bridge. The island boasted a large park donated by St. Paul's first public health officer, Dr. Justus Ohage, who had funded its well-used public bath. Elsewhere along the shore, a mix of Jewish, Italian, Mexican, and other young St. Paulites swam in the Mississippi during the hot summers, the city skyline serving as backdrop for splashing.

Like many low-lying neighborhoods, the river flats were prone to Mississippi River flooding. In 1952 a particularly large flood put homes and basements underwater, and cars were often unable to traverse the streets. The flood gave city leaders an opportunity to follow through on a long-standing idea: bulldozing and clearing the flats. As far back as 1917, urban reformers had proposed demolishing the community to boost the city economy: housing consultant Carol Aronovici wrote that "the 'flats' if properly treated would afford a splendid opportunity for the development of an industrial zone accessible to rail and river transportation instead of being what they are today, a slum of the worst character."

When urban renewal money became available, St. Paul's leaders seized the chance. Together, the Army Corps of Engineers, the St. Paul Port Authority (a quasi-governmental funding agency), and the city's housing authority proposed demolishing the "slum" and building a new industrial park, in hopes of attracting tax-paying industries—and thus lower city tax rates. In 1950 officials constructed a new river levee and filled in Harriet Island's back channel, making it an island in name only. At the same time, city officials condemned and demolished hundreds of homes and businesses on the flats, nearly every building. Homeowners were accorded some compensation, though not everyone was pleased with their offer. Renters were promised months of free rent to offset moving costs, but authorities later reneged on that promise. Meanwhile, a new affordable housing project was constructed farther south on the West Side, on higher ground, though even that project was fought by other St. Paul neighbors concerned about "moving the slum" south up the bluff.

According to historian Dennis Valdés, the Mississippi floods served as a handy excuse for the larger project of displacement and economic transformation. As he describes it, "'urban renewal' in the barrio demonstrates that city officials consciously conflated the story of the early 1950s floods, the flood control project, the industrial park, and the displacement of the Mexican *colonia*." A few years after the demolition, the new

The flooded West Side, east of Robert Street, in 1952

Riverview Industrial Park had rendered the old flats unrecognizable. Entire streets were missing, and the clearance forced over two thousand people to leave their homes, with barely a single structure remaining from the prewar era. On the West Side to this day, people exchange stories of relatives who refused to cash the checks they had received from the city, defiantly clinging to the memory of the old community.

St. Paul's most infamous urban renewal project arrived a few years later alongside freeway construction. Passage of the 1956 Federal-Aid Highway Act gave an opportunity for city planners to leverage federal money to achieve their goals. While most other countries used limited-access highways to connect cities, rarely building them through dense urban areas, the United States adopted a widespread practice of demolishing neighborhoods for urban highways. These massive projects often provided cover for plans aimed at so-called slum clearance. With the federal government paying 90 percent of the costs, city leaders could eliminate working-class neighborhoods with brand-new automobile infrastructure.

The freeway investments coincided neatly with the end of Twin City Rapid Transit (TCRT), the long-running streetcar system. At its peak, the Twin Cities had one of the country's best streetcar transit systems, with high-quality vehicles made and maintained in St. Paul. There were nine hundred streetcars running on over five hundred miles of track, providing more than two hundred million rides a year. But by the 1950s, the streetcar system was struggling with funding and competing with an exponential increase in car owners. Streetcar profits had always been closely tied to real estate development, as land deals had funded ongoing expenses. Without room to grow and facing ongoing maintenance costs and declining ridership, running a private streetcar company became a losing proposition. Without major government intervention, it was hard to see a future for the streetcars.

The last years of the streetcar system were also marked by scandal. The TCRT was bought by a few different investors, none of whom prioritized its long-term health, before Fred Ossanna, a local attorney with connections to the underworld mob, wound up running it. Working with a business cartel, he decided to convert the entire system to buses built by General Motors. By the mid-1950s, the streetcar rails were being covered with asphalt and the last streetcars were auctioned off or simply burned on-site. Ossanna was later convicted of fraud and conspiracy for selling parts of the system for below-market prices.

The end of the streetcars dramatically changed the landscape of downtown St. Paul and the commercial corridors that ran through the city. From then on, it was clear that automobiles would be the priority for city planners and federal dollars, while buses and rail transit were relegated to the margins of city streets or disappeared completely. For many people in St. Paul, the new freeway represented the future.

But where would it be located? In St. Paul, an internal debate broke out over the freeway location, pitting longtime St. Paul planning head George Herrold against a coalition of city boosters and state highway engineers. Herrold favored plans that minimized disruption to the city's neighborhoods, including building a grade-level boulevard, while state engineers favored a straight-line freeway route between downtown St. Paul and Minneapolis. The straighter proposal put the on-ramps closer to wealthier neighborhoods to the south, but it also meant constructing the highway through the middle of the Rondo community.

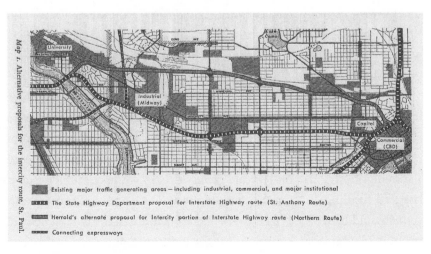

George Herrold's preferred route for I-94 ran north of most neighborhoods.

The core of St. Paul's Black community was a mile-wide stretch of homes and streets that centered on Rondo Avenue. Even by the standards of the skeptical housing appraisers, much of Rondo had relatively good housing stock and was in decent shape. And yet, because its residents were predominantly Black, the entire neighborhood area was coded as D / Failing on the 1930s maps, redlined and ineligible for federally subsidized mortgages. Like the Mexicans on the West Side, the thousands of Black people in St. Paul had few housing alternatives. Unable to get financing for homes in redlined areas and kept out of white neighborhoods by housing covenants and discrimination, Black families found it very hard to build up housing wealth. As a result, most Black St. Paulites lived in the small Rondo community, composed of the nicer Oatmeal Hill area to the west and the more working-class Cornmeal Valley to the east. Black people who crossed the invisible racial boundaries on Selby Avenue, Lexington Parkway, or University Avenue could be greeted with reactions ranging from indifference to hostility.

These geographic limitations, and the narrowed economic opportunities on the city's job market, meant Black people in St. Paul were hemmed in, literally and figuratively, a fact that made Rondo and other ethnic enclaves highly vulnerable to displacement. These de facto limits meant that the new intercity freeway route, right down the middle of Rondo and St. Anthony Avenues, would eviscerate St. Paul's Black community. This was the fate that George Herrold and St. Paul's Black community leaders wanted desperately to avoid.

Behind the scenes, the debate over the freeway route was over before it began. Herrold was the most prominent city voice opposing the Rondo route, and he argued for a northern alternative, paralleling the Burlington Northern railroad tracks and bypassing the Rondo and Merriam Park neighborhoods. Yet Herrold faced off against the combined expertise and funding clout of the state highway department. The northern route would be tricky to fit into the lucrative industrial trucking district in St. Paul's Midway. Herrold's last-ditch alternative, a less-destructive surface boulevard, would not qualify for the 90 percent federal funding subsidy and was a nonstarter. By 1956, the direct route through Rondo was selected, changing St. Paul forever.

As with other urban renewal projects aimed at working-class enclaves, there was little consultation or opportunity for pushback. State and city officials used eminent domain, and owners of homes or businesses were given checks, while those who refused to leave faced the eventual abandonment of their community. Rondo's renters got next to nothing.

By the early 1960s, the bulldozers had cleared away a large swath of one of St. Paul's oldest working-class communities. When Interstate 94 officially opened in 1968, freeway construction and associated urban renewal had demolished over six hundred family homes and businesses, including every building between St. Anthony and Rondo Avenues. As a last gesture, Rondo Avenue itself, renamed Concordia, was erased completely from the map.

While white people were also displaced by freeway construction and urban renewal programs, they retained the advantage of being able to live anywhere they could afford, and they could easily qualify for federally subsidized mortgages. For St. Paul's Black community, on the other hand, restarting was more difficult. Finding financing in redlined neighborhoods was a challenge, and many Black folks displaced from Rondo were forced by circumstance and discrimination to find shelter in unwelcoming neighborhoods. Over the next few years, African Americans increasingly moved to the neighboring Frogtown, Ramsey Hill, and Hamline-Midway areas. This movement was made easier by white flight, as white residents in older neighborhoods, like mostly German Frogtown, bought new homes in St. Paul suburbs.

The new central freeway, alongside many other highways and road expansions, fundamentally fragmented St. Paul. Old walkable neighborhoods were now bisected by wide roads full of cars and trucks speeding through the city to the fast-growing suburbs. The central freeway was the worst of them. The only concession that affected communities were able to wring from the project planners was that the highway be depressed below grade, instead of elevated on concrete, as initially proposed.

The saga of freeway construction in St. Paul stretched on for decades, and its course never did run smoothly. Most other freeways built through the central city ran along ravines and creek beds; for example, the freeway north from downtown (35E) occupied the ravine created by Trout Brook, buried in a tunnel in the 1880s. The new highway running south from downtown (US 52) again carved up the West Side neighborhood, though by then, few old homes remained.

St. Paul's last section of urban freeway system was the trickiest, the leg of the 35E freeway running southwest out of downtown. It was set to run along Pleasant Avenue, a residential street with stately homes along the base of the bluffs below Ramsey, Cathedral, and Crocus Hills. The street sat in the shadow of the Summit Avenue mansions, including James J. Hill's house, that continued to make St. Paul's urban skyline famous. More than most other neighborhoods that stood in the path of progress, the Pleasant Avenue and West End communities were well organized, and by 1972 they had seen enough freeway projects to recognize the significant downsides. Drawing on new environmental protection laws, a group of residents challenged the freeway planners' process, alleging that it had not accounted for environmental impacts to the community.

As a result of the lawsuit, the freeway construction stretched on for years. By the mid-1970s, as homes within the planned right-of-way had been acquired and demolished by city planners, there was little chance of actually preventing the freeway from coming through the Pleasant Avenue neighborhood. The lawsuit continued through years of legal wrangling, until a 1984 court order by a federal judge settled the issue, granting the neighbors a number of concessions. A bike path would be built alongside the south wall of the project, trucks would be banned from the stretch of interstate (rather tragically, as it forced many of them to drive on city streets instead), and the speed limit would be set at forty-five miles per hour. The final leg of St. Paul's central freeway network finally opened in 1990, and all three conditions are still in place, much to the chagrin of both truckers and Minnesota speeders.

The opening of the final urban freeway marked the end of St. Paul's great postwar transformation, which saw entire neighborhoods vanish, replaced with highways fueling suburban growth. The new St. Paul, driven by huge postwar federal investments, was radically different from the old, leaving behind only pockets of the nineteenth-century landscape. Indeed, many of the demolished neighborhoods of the bulldozer era have been all but forgotten. Pleasant Avenue is barely marked on city maps, and there's almost no trace of the old Central Park or Fourteenth Street neighborhoods around the state capitol. The West Side Flats fared little better, the old streets removed from the map in favor of wide roads and still-vacant lots. Instead, the community is kept alive in the memories of residents who still rue the day that the city took their parents' homes. A wooden model of the old community remains on display in the lobby of the Neighborhood House, a settlement house and nonprofit that's been educating and helping working-class people on the West Side for over a century.

Likewise, the residents of St. Paul's Rondo neighborhood managed to keep the spirit of the old community alive. In 1983, a group of people who remembered what it was like before the freeway began celebrating Rondo Days, an annual festival and parade to commemorate the historic community. Over the years, the festival grew into an annual celebration of St. Paul's Black heritage, tinged with the recognition of what has been lost through the years of discrimination and city-led injustice.

In July 2015, over sixty years after the first bulldozer came through, the commissioner of the state Department of Transportation and the then-mayor of St. Paul officially apologized to Rondo residents for the freeway construction. "American freeways tended to twist and curve to avoid wealthy neighborhoods and then straightened out into swaths of destruction through the neighborhoods of the poor, the disenfranchised, and the nonwhite," admitted Mayor Chris Coleman that day. Since then, a small community plaza has been built near what was once Rondo Avenue. If you visit it today, you'll see a display of some of the history of the old community while you listen to the constant roar of traffic coming from the freeway a few feet away.

CHAPTER 7

Resilience

Such snug urban enclaves were just then eroding. The children of
these tight, tender old neighborhoods were taking to the urban
margins, to what, years later, we would call sprawl. . . . The Italians
were departing in a drastically biblical way, flooded out. . . . For years
after that, the rest of my girlhood and beyond, the levee was given over
to a scrap-metal yard where smashed and flattened cars lay stacked like
cords of firewood for a colossal bonfire that was never lit. From time to
time bands of homeless people set up temporary camps along the
riverbanks in the warm months—and were eventually hounded out.
The river became the disdained territory of throwaways, used-up objects,
discarded people.

—Patricia Hampl, *The Florist's Daughter*

One pleasant thing about the ball field at Cretin-Derham High School
is that the outfield wall is just feet from the sidewalk. On a summer's
day, anyone can wander down Randolph Avenue and watch a ball game
played by one of the state's best high school teams. Coming out of the
ice cream shop or the barber, anyone can mingle with cheering family
members, watch a home run fly over Hamline Avenue, or even fetch a
foul ball to return to the umpire. This kind of interactive tradition—a
mix of recreation, culture, and community that forms the fiber of everyday city life—has been passed down for generations in St. Paul. Helped
by a strong park system, St. Paul has worked to keep social connections
thriving through some of the twentieth century's turbulent years.

Baseball in particular has played a strong role. It's unusual for a midwestern city to boast three Baseball Hall of Famers, with another one
on the way—Dave Winfield, Paul Molitor, Jack Morris, and (mark my

words) Joe Mauer—and the city's identity is tied to America's pastime. Since 1939, during the long off-season, former players, fans, and umpires have met monthly at a local bar to discuss baseball history and prepare for the coming season. Meetings of the Baseball Old Timers Hot Stove League moved around town for decades before finding a back room of a Frogtown bar whose walls were covered with photos of early St. Paul teams, including framed pictures of the company nines from places like Crex Furniture, the Unique Theater, or American Hoist and Derrick. Through the years, the group evolved alongside the city's Catholic schools, the park system, and amateur leagues, all of which helped baseball thrive in St. Paul.

Not far away, the city's pro team, the St. Paul Saints, played for years at a ballpark on the corner of Lexington and University, just on the

Roy Campanella
at the Lexington
Ballpark, 1948

edge of the Rondo neighborhood. The Saints were the farm team for the Chicago White Sox (1936–42), then the Dodgers (Brooklyn, 1944–57; Los Angeles, 1958–60), and many famous players stopped in St. Paul on their way up. In 1948, the big name was Roy Campanella, a young veteran of the Negro and Mexican leagues who was one of the first African Americans to make the majors, alongside Jackie Robinson. He broke the color barrier with the Saints, hitting thirteen home runs and playing catcher in St. Paul before heading east to the show.

Yet locally, Campanella is not St. Paul's most famous Negro Leaguer. That honor goes instead to Toni Stone, a little-known name outside St. Paul, but the first and only woman to play in the Negro Leagues alongside the men. Stone grew up on the streets of Rondo, where she excelled at games like red rover and baseball, never backing down from a challenge and insisting to coaches that she compete with anyone. As a teenage tomboy, Stone played with the Twin Cities Colored Giants before her two seasons in the Negro Leagues, where she skipped around from New Orleans to Kansas City to Indianapolis, keeping a .243 average while turning double plays, digging into the box, and constantly dealing with sexism. Today, a field named for her sits next to Central High School, just across the freeway from where the Saints once played.

St. Paul is also a hockey town, and since the 1973 construction of the Civic Center arena it has hosted the Minnesota State High School hockey tournament. The competition remains an annual rite for the state's best teenage skaters and stick handlers, alongside their friends, classmates, and obsessive parents. For generations, frozen lakes have been cleared and city parks and vacant lots flooded so that neighborhood kids could skate and scrimmage through the winter. St. Paul's most famous hockey alumnus was an East Sider named Herb Brooks, who grew up playing on rinks around Johnson High School in the 1950s, leading his school to a state championship. Brooks then played for the Gophers and made the Olympic teams in '64 and '68 before coaching Gophers hockey for years. Famously, Brooks coached the underdog US Olympic team in 1980 in the "Miracle on Ice," their defeat of the Soviet Union at Lake Placid, New York.

Brooks was one of dozens of professional hockey players and coaches who got their start in St. Paul, a city that, thanks in part to the annual winter carnival, has long prided itself on cold weather competition. The same can be said for the St. Paul Curling Club on Selby Avenue, which dates back to the winter carnival in 1885. The clubhouse, built in 1912, has hosted hundreds of bonspiels over the years on the rinks on Selby Avenue, through the ups and downs of an obscure sport. Since curling became an Olympic sport in 1998, the Selby Avenue club has been the home base for more than one American medalist.

St. Paul boasted lower-brow athletic glory in its thriving professional wrestling scene. Thanks to the local connections of famous promoter Vern Gagne, St. Paul's downtown Civic Center hosted countless marquee matches of the biggest names in the Minneapolis-based American Wrestling Association circuit. Throughout the 1980s, after a match, wrestlers like Hulk Hogan, André the Giant, and many others would often head down the street to the back rooms at Mancini's Char House, the famous steak joint started by Italians who moved up from the demolished river flats. Bartenders still tell stories of asking inebriated wrestlers—André was over seven feet tall and five hundred pounds—to go home after the restaurant closed down at night, which was surely an unenviable task.

St. Paul's sports traditions remained strong despite the dramatic changes of the twentieth century's last decades. Displacement from urban renewal and freeway construction combined with conflicts over civil rights and America's wars to finally bring segregation and inequality into the social spotlight. The growth of nearly all-white suburban cities and the increased diversification of older urban neighborhoods were both transforming St. Paul's old boundaries of race and class. On the one hand, new rapidly expanding cities like Roseville, Maplewood, West St. Paul, and Oakdale grew on the edge of St. Paul, with new subdivisions full of ranch homes, attached garages, culs-de-sac, shopping centers, and de facto segregated schools unsettling the social landscape of the east metro. As more suburbs grew around the highways, commercial strips, and parking lots, the political gravity shifted. The new landscape changed old St. Paul, which no longer competed with Minneapolis for jobs, population, housing, or government funding. Instead, St. Paul was fighting for growth against suburban enclaves on all sides.

Like most US cities in the late twentieth century, St. Paul lost population thanks to suburbanization, job loss, and the lack of investment in older neighborhoods. City population peaked between 1950 and 1970, plateauing at just over 310,000 and declining after that. It could have been worse: Minneapolis lost 40 percent of its peak population to the suburbs, while St. Paul stayed relatively steady, with just a 20 percent drop. Part of St. Paul's stability lay in its strong traditions and neighborhoods, especially the Catholic parishes, centered on churches and schools. On top of that, beginning in the mid-1970s, a steady stream of immigration flowed into St. Paul from around the world, helping offset the ongoing flight to the suburbs.

Yet the loss of population was not helped along by the erosion of jobs from city borders, as industry and offices alike decamped for literal greener pastures. In 1962, one of the city's largest employers, 3M, moved its headquarters from its East Side complex to a sprawling new campus over the border in suburban Maplewood. The departure was just the beginning. Over the next decades, jobs fled the East Side thanks to corporate consolidation, automation, and mergers. Employment at the massive Whirlpool (formerly Seeger) Refrigerator factory dwindled during the 1970s and '80s before it finally shut down for good in 1984. Facing increased competition from macro brewers in Wisconsin and Missouri, the city's two large beer companies fell on hard times beginning in the 1970s. The venerable Hamm's was sold to a competitor, Detroit-based Stroh's, but production declined again before it closed for good in 1997.

The West End's Schmidt Brewery lasted a bit longer, thanks to dogged efforts by city leaders to keep it in the neighborhood. When Schmidt was sold to a Wisconsin company, a St. Paul group managed to reboot the brewery under new brands called Landmark and Pig's Eye—a charming nod to the old moniker—until they, too, finally shut down in 2002. (For a while afterward, the old brewery served as an ethanol factory, until the stench from the distillation proved to be too much for the neighbors.) In general, globalization, increased competition, automation, and the lure of subsidized land in suburbia made jobs hard to find in St. Paul and shifted the economic center of gravity away from the city.

Meanwhile, downtown St. Paul had become a bit of an economic backwater, and its future was uncertain. The new freeways formed a moat around the old office core, which was already hemmed in on the east by the high bluff, railroad tracks, and the Trout Brook valley. Though urban renewal removed some older buildings in need of rehabilitation, the new roads destroyed a huge percentage of the traditional center, replacing it with parking lots, on-ramps, and truck routes along the waterfront. Downtown's isolation posed major problems for the old retail giants, which had once been the epicenter of regional shopping. The old city had been full of department stores. The high-end Field-Schlick boutique on Fifth Street offered fine cosmetics, crystal, and linens and an expensive dress subscription service. The Golden Rule stood a few blocks away, St. Paul's largest and oldest department store. It dated back to 1896 and had once featured hundreds of employees selling everything under the sun. Across Seventh Street was the five-story Emporium, boasting a tearoom, hundreds of ever-changing hats, and a wide variety of home goods and clothing. Across the street was Rothschild's, a branch of a famous high-end Chicago clothier. A few blocks away, on Sixth and

St. Paul Chamber Orchestra / Schubert Club

Downtown St. Paul has long hosted some of the state's finest cultural and media institutions, including Twin Cities Public Television, Minnesota Public Radio and the Fitzgerald Theater (longtime home of Garrison Keillor's *A Prairie Home Companion* radio show), the Minnesota Historical Society, the Science Museum of Minnesota, and the Minnesota Museum of American Art. Thousands of people come downtown to visit these ever-changing institutions, which keep history and culture at the forefront of city conversation.

St. Paul is rich in musical history as well, and one of its oldest music groups dates back at least to 1882. That year, some German-speaking community organizers, led by Marion Ramsey Furness, the daughter of

Alexander Ramsey, formed the Schubert Club. The group began organiz-ing recitals and musical events to share culture from Bavaria, Austria, and other parts of northern Europe. Over the years, the club evolved into an ongoing musical society, hosting performances and operating a museum of nineteenth-century instruments in the Landmark Center (the old fed-eral courthouse).

The Schubert Club's success set the tone for the city's flagship classi-cal music group, the St. Paul Chamber Orchestra (SPCO). The orchestra dates to the 1950s, when city leaders were struggling to find ways to ensure that crowds kept coming downtown. In 1959, some St. Paul music fans launched the new chamber orchestra, aimed at being smaller and more flexible than the large symphony in Minneapolis. At the SPCO's first concert, held in the Central High School auditorium, Leopold Sipe directed music by Purcell, Bach, and Mozart. For the next decade, the thirty-three-member group performed throughout the Upper Midwest, and within ten years they played to plaudits at Carnegie Hall.

Over the years, the SPCO featured a wide range of well-known music, artistic, and creative directors, people like Dennis Russell Davies, Hugh Wolff, Pinchas Zukerman, and Bobby McFerrin. Because of its smaller size, the SPCO even proved an ideal choice for touring beyond the Iron Curtain during the Cold War, and the group performed throughout East-ern Europe and the Soviet Union in 1974 and 1975. In 1985, led by the philanthropic efforts of Sally Ordway Irvine, an heir to the 3M fortune, the orchestra moved from a theater on Cedar Street into the Ordway Center for the Arts, a new downtown concert hall on Rice Park. Over the years, the orchestra has won two Grammy awards.

As with most orchestras in the pop era, there have been difficult times. In 1993, nearby Minnesota Public Radio hosted an SOS ("Save Our SPCO") telethon, raising $700,000 to keep the orchestra from insolvency. In 2012, facing a huge budget shortfall, SPCO management locked out its union musicians until a contract with pay cuts was finally adopted the next year. Today, over sixty years after it began, the SPCO continues to perform in the downtown Hamm Building, the Ordway, and small ven-ues through the state, bringing European art music to a wide audience.

Dennis Russell Davies conducts a rehearsal of the St. Paul Chamber Orchestra
in the atrium of the Landmark Center, about 1980.

Wabasha, sat Schuneman's, another homegrown department store dating back to 1890.

None of these stores would last much longer. Schuneman's was the
first to go, torn down in 1963 when a massive new store was built across
the street by the Minneapolis retailer Dayton's. The new Dayton's was
designed by the retail guru Victor Gruen, who had also designed the
pioneering Southdale Mall in Edina; both are self-contained and win-
dowless. The Golden Rule was bought by a different Minneapolis competitor, Donaldson's, in 1961; the Emporium closed in 1968, and Field's
shuttered in 1979.

The new Dayton's store made up but one part of a larger transformation planned for central downtown. Called the Capital Centre project, it
was an ambitious effort to modernize downtown to compete with both
the suburbs and Minneapolis. In practice, that meant clearing blocks
of historic buildings for new, superblock office towers. As a result, the
sixties saw blocks of old brick shops, offices, hotels, and apartments

Dayton's Department Store at Fifth and Cedar, about 1975

demolished and large modern towers constructed in their place. Just as
Minneapolis had done years earlier, St. Paul's new urban planners linked
the office towers with second-story skyways, intended to protect workers
from the weather but, in effect, segregating the downtown population
along race and class lines. The main difference between the two cities'
skyway systems was that St. Paul's was built using public dollars; each
bridge matched a standardized design and was technically public space,
regulated by the city. In practice, the distinction did not much matter.

Out were the small, varied brick buildings of the old downtown. In
were the gray, concrete modernist towers. Linked by skyways, the new
buildings turned inward to create a city within the city, a mall-like space
of offices and lunch spots in the midst of the old downtown, nearly every
shop catering solely to the nine-to-five office crowd. The most elegant
of them still is the gleaming modernist Osborn370 tower (formerly the
Ecolab headquarters), its large plaza on Wabasha Street adorned with a
shiny abstract sculpture.

The new Dayton's store was built around a large internal parking garage and connected seamlessly to the city's skyway system. For many people, the department icon remained the most popular part of the St. Paul skyways. Yet, in 1970, the St. Paul Dayton's suffered a catastrophe. The store was the site of a bombing in a flashpoint of racial unrest in St. Paul at the time. Fueled by racial tensions and anti–Vietnam War anxiety, a fifteen-year-old St. Paul kid named Gary Hogan planted a stick of dynamite in a women's bathroom one Saturday evening. Around 5 PM, it exploded, destroying two toilets and injuring a high school teacher who was combing her hair. A second, much larger bomb was discovered in a locker by an alert security guard. Had it gone off, it would likely have killed dozens of first responders and reporters.

The Dayton's bombing was a symptom of the larger racial conflicts that had plagued St. Paul, and most northern cities, from the beginning. These tensions were coming to the foreground in the late 1960s. Rising crime rates and disinvestment, alongside the added pressure on the community following the destruction of the historic Rondo corridor, made the city's former racial seams into pressure points for simmering tensions.

In 1968, following the assassination of Dr. Martin Luther King Jr. in Memphis, Selby Avenue because the site of the worst racial unrest in city history. Heated by the divisive politics of the era and the effects of long-standing structural racism, St. Paul boiled over. In the worst incident, one August night St. Paul police raided an R&B concert at downtown's Stem Hall, where a nearly all-Black audience was dancing and enjoying the music inside. When some minor conflicts involving off-duty police on a security detail got out of hand outside the venue, a group of white police officers barricaded the doors of the building, shot tear gas inside, and hit young people with nightsticks during the commotion. Because of the violent incident, upset community members demonstrated for days afterward against ongoing police racism and social inequality. In the ensuing unrest, many of Selby Avenue's small businesses—barbershops, delis, grocers, and a printer—were vandalized or set on fire. For years afterward, the historic commercial strip along Selby Avenue languished as businesses began to shut their doors.

The sense of neighborhoods as racial turf was a two-way street, and other areas of St. Paul remained proudly all-white. As a memoir written by a Black police officer described it, through the 1970s, neighborhoods like the North End's Rice Street were known as places where Black people were unwelcome: "When I was growing up, we all knew to stay off of Rice, or to zip through fast and not stop. It was entirely off-limits for all Blacks. Now [in the 1970s], as Black communities expanded, racial tensions soared."

Even as some parts of St. Paul entered a cycle of disinvestment and economic struggle, federal projects channeled investments into underserved communities in other parts of town. By the early 1970s, the shift to Community Development Block Grants allowed city leaders to more precisely target investments according to community input. Millions of federal dollars were spent in areas like Summit-University to rehab old houses, build affordable housing, and establish hubs like the new Hallie Q. Brown Community Center. Just off Marshall Avenue, the center houses a space for community gatherings alongside a gym and recreation site. It also is home to the Penumbra Theatre, founded in 1976 to produce plays that reflect the African American experience. The Penumbra, the largest African American theater in the United States, was first to produce several works by two-time Pulitzer Prize–winner August Wilson, who wrote several of his plays while living in St. Paul. Elsewhere in St. Paul, public housing programs built less dense affordable housing facilities amid the former urban renewal areas, though getting maintenance support from the federal government continues to be extremely difficult. While demand far outpaces funding for subsidized housing in St. Paul, projects that were built, like the McDonough or Mount Airy Homes, remain lifelines for generations of families moving to St. Paul.

During the difficult period of the late 1960s and early 1970s, the concept of historic preservation was beginning to impact St. Paul's older communities around the cathedral. One of the city's earliest efforts took

place on Ramsey Hill, which in 1973 became the largest preservation
district in the country. Drawing on city funding, hundreds of homes
and condos were rehabbed in historic neighborhoods around Summit
and Selby Avenues, helping the mostly white residents who were returning to the area that had been partially abandoned by the city's wealthier
classes a generation before. Throughout the 1980s and '90s, supported
by a heaping of sweat equity, public and private restoration efforts ensured
that Victorian-era homes on the hill would survive into the future.

At the same time that the diverse Selby Avenue area struggled, Grand
Avenue, a largely white commercial corridor a half mile to the south,
became one of St. Paul's economic development success stories. A long
mixed-use street that had once featured a well-used streetcar, Grand
Avenue was just one block off Summit Avenue and had been transforming for years. As far back as the 1920s, the street was home to many of
the dealerships of St. Paul's first big automobile boom, when dozens of
companies hawked motorcars to the city's upper classes. As car culture

Selby Avenue, 1967

shifted and grew, most auto enterprises moved away, and Grand Avenue's old showrooms remained behind, slowly declining or becoming repair garages. By the 1970s, the avenue's identity shifted again as entrepreneurs and small-business people moved into the old spaces to start shops and service industries catering to the city's white middle class.

In 1974, the street's fortunes got a boost when entrepreneurs hosted a parade and festival traversing the length of the avenue. Within a few years the event, which became known as Grand Old Day, had proved a wild success and attracted thousands of people each year to the merchants of old St. Paul. By 1984, one of St. Paul's first high-end coffee shops, Cafe Latte, opened up in an old Studebaker dealership at Grand and Victoria, long before Starbucks had made espresso a household word. The café was one of dozens of shops that followed, and soon enough it was clear that St. Paul's urban fabric could forge a new model of modern retail, an alternative to malls in the suburbs. There was still demand for the urban experience, and places like Grand Avenue might attract white suburbanites craving diversity and street life.

St. Paul's late-twentieth-century flexibility was helped by political shifts in city hall, especially changes to the long-standing commission system of city governance. Ever since 1912, the city's elected officials had operated through an antiquated political structure whereby city council members, elected in citywide elections, were given charge of specific city departments—Public Works, Planning, or Finance—which led to some awkwardly incompetent governance over the years. The system also ensured that elected officials almost always reflected the city's wealthiest and highest-turnout populations, mirroring white, middle-class political sentiments. Winning seats against the often Irish and German mainstream culture was a rare thing. If anything, occasional exceptions, like long-serving Jewish city council member Milton Rosen, proved the rule.

Though it was certainly neither inclusive nor efficient, St. Paul's commission system had some benefits. For example, according to one political analysis, there was "virtually no patronage" in St. Paul when compared to the big city machines like Chicago or Philadelphia. On the other hand, the lack of governmental spoils may have been an illusion, papered over by the intimate relationship between officials and their workers. Because St. Paul's officials had de facto control over single departments, they were able to use city services for personal purposes. For example, one commissioner was notorious for abusing city garages for personal car repairs. Meanwhile, the city budget was almost completely controlled by a comptroller, a separate elected official who maintained a long-standing practice of keeping property taxes as low as possible. Supported by St. Paul's ever-thrifty business community, one comptroller named Joe Mitchell served from 1942 to 1970, reelected each time on the promise of keeping the size of government at a minimum.

St. Paul's static politics began to change in the 1960s, especially when a colorful Summit Avenue woman named Rosalie Butler began attending city council meetings. Driven and combative, Butler often brought with her reams of supposed testimony and evidence of city corruption. Accurate or not, her accusations received a lot of press attention, and eventually earned her a council seat of her own. Other reform-minded advocates were pushing plans for a new strong mayor governance system. The proposal would separate elected officials from the legislative function of overseeing city staff, while removing the limits and influence of the powerful comptroller.

In 1972, voters passed a referendum to make the changes, moving the city to a geographic ward-based city council with a strong mayor, who would be more able to take civic action. The new approach consolidated power and budgetary control in the mayor's office, which, for better or for worse, helped St. Paul get more aggressive with urban projects. These powers proved especially helpful for the longest-serving mayor in city history, George Latimer, a lawyer from upstate New York who held office from 1976 to 1990. At least in theory, the new politics of St. Paul allowed government to put together funding packages, budgets, and regulatory approval more swiftly than other, more complicated systems, like the one in Minneapolis.

In the beginning, much of St. Paul's newfound civic attention was turned toward downtown, which struggled to stay relevant in the fast-changing Twin Cities. Throughout the seventies and eighties, all kinds of big ideas were pitched at city leaders. The most elaborate may have been a mid-1970s vision for a downtown "people mover" monorail. Drawing on a short-lived pot of federal money, St. Paul's new train would be loosely based on similar elevated transit in Miami and Detroit. The focal point would be a massive skyway-centered urban mall called Town Square, taking up a whole downtown block. The monorail train would then run in a Y-shaped route above the sidewalks of St. Paul, connecting the skyways of the office core with the state capitol, the Civic Center arena, and a hospital on the edge of the old Seven Corners neighborhood.

Thankfully for urbanists, the people mover was never funded or built, as most similar transit projects have proved to be failures. Yet the downtown Town Square building was constructed, and it still stands today— though the elaborate glass-roofed skyway park that was its centerpiece is now cordoned off and mothballed, waiting for the next grand downtown dream. Still other municipal projects of the 1980s were far more successful, especially the construction of downtown's environmentally efficient district energy system.

While leaders were hatching big development schemes, historic preservation played a contrasting role in the eventual rebound of downtown, ensuring that not all of the city's historic buildings were torn down in the name of progress. The earliest preservation success was an effort to rescue the historic federal courthouse, the immense turreted Richardsonian Romanesque structure on the north edge of Rice Park. By the late 1960s, the future Landmark Center was marked for demolition, slated to become a convenient parking lot between the shopping district and the nearby arena. It would have become the latest in a string of architectural casualties that gutted the city's nineteenth-century legacy after they were viewed as unsalvageable and largely worthless: the 1882 Ryan Hotel (torn down in 1962), 1887 Globe Building (torn down in 1959), or the 1889 New York Life Building (torn down in 1967). Instead, history and preservation advocates banded together and persuaded the county to purchase the courthouse property, eventually rehabbing it into an event center and home for nonprofits and museums like the Schubert Club and the Ramsey County Historical Society.

Mayor George Latimer in Town Square, about 1980

By the 1970s, as more people in St. Paul began to value historic buildings, a nascent preservation movement gelled alongside efforts to revitalize urban economies. The next big project, after the success of the
Ramsey Hill restorations, was the run-down Lowertown neighborhood,
the large collection of late-nineteenth-century warehouse buildings on
the eastern edge of downtown. Thanks to the attention of historians and
artists, the Lowertown area was declared a historic district in 1983, and
since then has evolved more than once, becoming homes and studios
for artists, loft apartments, restaurants, coffee shops, and art galleries at
the edge of downtown St. Paul.

Demolition of the Globe Building at 115 East Sixth Street, 1959

Though professional baseball in St. Paul disappeared in 1961, when the Minnesota Twins arrived in suburban Bloomington, the sport would not abandon the city forever. Partly in response to long-simmering disgust at the indoor baseball in the eighties-era Metrodome stadium, in 1993 an entrepreneur named Bill Veeck launched a new amateur baseball team in St. Paul, rebooting the city's historic minor-league franchise. The unaffiliated St. Paul Saints played teams from Fargo, Winnipeg, and Rochester at Midway Stadium, located just off the railroad tracks at the edge of the city's industrial district. The inelegant ballpark, where the omnipresent freight trains rattled down the BNSF line, served as a background for the historic blue-and-white Saints uniforms. Marketing themselves with the slogan "Fun is good," the team began to bring fans into St. Paul to watch professional baseball in the sunshine.

If you go to a game today, you'll find that the Saints play in a new stadium in Lowertown and are newly affiliated with the Minnesota Twins as a AAA-level club. Constructed in 2014, and helped along by targeted

St. Paul Saints at Midway Stadium, 1993

city dollars, the ballpark was designed by a local architect to blend in neatly with the historic nineteenth-century warehouses. Tucked in behind the sixties-era freeways that ring the city's center, the ballpark brings fans into downtown to experience the mix of traditions and shenanigans, old and new, that have kept St. Paul connected and thriving for years.

CHAPTER 8

Renaissance

When I stepped close to a table lined with low white boxes filled with
an array of baked goods and saw my very first glazed doughnuts, when
the woman standing behind them smiled at me and offered me a
thumb-size bite on a toothpick, my mouth fell open and my eyes filled
with gratitude. . . . When I put that bit of doughnut in my mouth, I knew
I would love the St. Paul Farmers' Market for as long as I lived, until the
very day I died, and maybe even beyond. The doughnut melted in my
mouth when I pressed my wet tongue against it. It was sweet and soft,
a little dry, perfect for me.

My mother pulled lightly on my cousin-in-law's arm. She gestured to
the dark-haired vendors who looked very Hmong to me.

My mother whispered, "Hmong farmers sell here?"

My cousin-in-law laughed, "Yes! Hmong farmers sell here. . . . Their
greens are the best. Even the white people know to come to their tables
to find the plumpest eggplants and biggest cabbages."

—Kao Kalia Yang, "Farmers Market Memories," 2020

By some accounts, the first Hmong refugees to arrive in St. Paul were
Leng Vang, May Ia Lee, and their family, who flew to the Twin Cities
airport from a refugee camp in Thailand in February 1976. When they
arrived in Minnesota, Hmong families were fleeing Laotian government
repression at the end of the so-called Secret War, an outgrowth of the
last years of the Vietnam War, which was then drawing to a close as a
disaster for all sides. Vang and Lee wound up in Minnesota thanks in
part to 1970s-era rules that required local sponsors, who would provide
better support for refugees in their new surroundings. The first Hmong
in St. Paul were sponsored by Minnesota churches and religious groups
like Catholic Charities and Lutheran Social Service. Beginning in the

1980s, regulations changed to allow secondary and family migration, starting a wave of Hmong immigration to St. Paul that would revitalize the city.

Before the late 1970s, few people in St. Paul had heard of the Hmong. As one refugee described it, "When we arrived here, they thought we were Vietnamese, so they started talking to us and asking us what part of Vietnam we were from. And I said, 'We're Hmong, and we're from Laos.' And they said, 'Where is Laos, and who are Hmong?'"

Hmong people are an ethnic group originally from the hills of southern China, and they retained distinct identity, traditions, and language in the mountains and upland areas of Southeast Asian countries like Vietnam, Laos, Cambodia, Myanmar, China, and Thailand. Hmong people were renowned for their skills in guerrilla combat, and during the Vietnam War the CIA recruited key Hmong leaders to assist Americans fighting the North Vietnamese, who were running supply lines through Laos and Cambodia. With US support, Hmong people fought for years before the war came to an end. When the US withdrew, it left most of the American allies in peril.

Many Hmong were persecuted and fled for their lives. The most common escape route was across the Mekong River into refugee camps in Thailand, whose government hosted Hmong people coming to the United States. Like millions who came to the United States before them, Hmong refugees sought the connections and comforts of friends, family, and kin, arriving in St. Paul to make a new home. At the same time, refugees fleeing persecution often carry additional burdens of trauma.

Most Hmong arrived without much knowledge of Minnesota beyond basics about the United States taught at the refugee camp—"hello," "thank you," etc.—and given the language, cultural, and financial barriers, the new city posed challenges. Despite being stunned by the cold weather, within a few years St. Paul's Hmong population had grown into one of the largest in the world, a community offering the material and kinship relationships that form the backbone of Hmong society. As one refugee remembered, "We couldn't understand the language. The fortunate thing for us Hmong was that we had relatives who came before.

It was harder for the ones who came first, but because of them it became easier for those who came afterwards." Hmong refugees brought with them rich cultural traditions in farming, music, and religion that made festivals, funerals, and weddings into grand events.

As in Laos, the highlight of the Hmong calendar is the New Year, an annual get-together for Hmong of all generations. Traditionally a festival that takes place at the end of the harvest, the weeklong New Year celebration usually occurs in November or December. Young men and women meet and court with a traditional ball toss game (alongside more conventionally American tactics) while families and adults share stories, music, dancing, and food. The Hmong tradition evolved and grew in the 1980s into an annual celebration in St. Paul, highlighted by a pageant, traditional clothing, folk songs, and religious ceremonies.

These days, around sixty thousand Hmong live in Minnesota, the large majority in and around St. Paul. While many Hmong arrivals first lived in multifamily or subsidized housing complexes, by the turn of the twenty-first century over half of Hmong households owned homes in neighborhoods like Frogtown, Summit-University, the North End, and throughout the East Side. All over the city, Hmong St. Paulites have been fixing up homes, gardening in backyards, and bringing a new vital culture to the city's neighborhoods. An additional annual event takes place in St. Paul: the Hmong International Freedom Festival, a sports tournament held in Como Park on July 4. It commemorates freedom in the United States, and thousands of Hmong Americans fill Como's athletic fields, competing in soccer, football, and other sports while enjoying food and the company of friends and family.

In some ways, Hmong immigration to St. Paul repeated a pattern that had been going on for generations. One initial tie that connected so many refugees from Southeast Asia, Latin America, and Africa to the city was the International Institute of Minnesota, founded in 1919 to help new immigrants in St. Paul. In the 1930s, the institute focused on helping Eastern European and Mexican immigrants gain a better understanding of their new homes, and on pushing back against commonplace anti-immigrant stereotypes and prejudices. To that end, beginning in

Ball toss at Hmong New Year celebration, Highland High School, 1981

1934, the International Institute hosted an annual celebration of cultural pluralism, a festival of diversity. According to one of the organizers, the festival was designed to give confidence to new immigrants and encourage understanding of difference. As she put it, reflecting progressive beliefs at the time, the festival helped change the culture of the city: "Diversity is coming to be looked on as an asset rather than a liability. Alien-baiting newspaper releases are not headlined in St. Paul papers. . . . If any person were now to express publicly [these] ideas in St. Paul, I believe, they would find voices in every audience refuting his contention."

The organization evolved over time, and its annual celebration came to be called the Festival of Nations, a display of folk dancing, food, and traditional dress of ethnic communities new and old. On one hand, the festival subsumed ethnic and racial difference into a melting pot celebration, giving short shrift to Native and marginalized groups, particularly Dakota, Ojibwe, and African Americans. On the other, the event fostered acceptance and recognition of new cultures. During World War II,

Festival of Nations, held during the statehood centennial in 1958

for example, the institute worked to ensure that Japanese American Nisei, members of the second generation who had been brought to the Midwest from California, were treated kindly, despite the rampant anti-Asian propaganda of the time. The festival still takes place each year, with people from many cultures sharing their stories of living in St. Paul alongside immigrant and refugee communities of past generations.

The arrival of Hmong to St. Paul offers the most significant example of how migration has shifted the city's demographics over the last forty years. Similar immigration and migration from places all over the country and world deeply changed St. Paul, bringing new vitality to its older commercial streets. In the late 1990s, photographer Wing Young Huie, who grew up in Duluth, described the vibrant experience of St. Paul's Frogtown neighborhood, which lies along University Avenue for two miles: "I turned a corner and was struck by the sight of a mélange of families, all on the same block—Asian, black, and white—out on their respective porches enjoying the day. And there were children everywhere, spilling out from the curbless sidewalks into the street. Then I saw a nun in a full white habit, walking through this jumble of life like an angel, or an aberration. It was intoxicating to witness such an exotic mix in such commonplace surroundings. I felt as though I had discovered a strange new territory."

Alongside the small businesses that had long served the city's Black community, by the 1990s dozens of shops owned by Asian American entrepreneurs had opened on University. On any given block you could find Thai restaurants serving luscious soup and noodle dishes, Vietnamese banh mi bakeries, or pho cafés where families gathered around big steaming bowls of broth, meat, bean sprouts, and basil leaves. Meanwhile, bars and restaurants like the Frogtown Diner or Porky's Drive-In catered to the avenue's car culture legacy. On weekend nights, white men driving American hot rods intermingled with the souped-up Japanese coupes that were the pride of St. Paul's Asian American car buffs. People

In Frogtown, about 1993. *Wing Young Huie*

cruised up and down the avenue past rows of street rods with their hoods raised, and St. Paul's cultural mix was on full display.

Elsewhere in St. Paul, similar transformations took place. By the turn of the twenty-first century, the East Side was home to large communities of people from Latin America, with streets like East Seventh and Payne Avenue featuring Mexican and Central American markets, stores, restaurants, and cultural centers hosting everything from quinceañeras to salsa dance nights. Other people making their home in St. Paul came from the Horn of Africa as Ethiopian, Oromo, Somali, and Eritrean refugees left political turmoil in their native countries. They brought with them both Muslim and Christian cultures, and entrepreneurs opened East African restaurants, coffee shops, and halal markets all over town. Much like the people who came before them, new Minnesotans started businesses and cultural centers, often in community mosques, markets, cafés, and coffee shops, reusing historic buildings in new ways. Both the Snelling-University area and the West Seventh and Shepard Road neighborhoods have become centers for East African immigrants to build community, creating a dynamic new center of activity and growth in St. Paul.

Wakaŋ Tipi

The Dakota were exiled from their homeland in 1862, and many of their descendants now live on Dakota reservations in South Dakota, Nebraska, and North Dakota, as well as Dakota reserves in Canada. In the 1880s, the federal government purchased land for four Dakota communities, recognizing the needs of Dakota people still living in the state. The closest of these to Bdote are the Shakopee Mdewakanton Sioux Community and the Prairie Island Indian Community, though a community of non-recognized Dakota remains at Mendota, not far from St. Paul's Highland Park neighborhood.

Nationally, over half of Native Americans live in cities, and St. Paul and its surroundings are no exception. Thousands of American Indian and Alaska Native people—about one percent of the population—live in and around St. Paul. The flag of the Mille Lacs Band of Ojibwe flies atop the Intercontinental Hotel, which is owned by the band, across the street from city hall. Meanwhile, the Prairie Island Mdewakanton Sioux flag can be seen three blocks away atop the Treasure Island Center, the remodeled Dayton's department store. Both demonstrate the ongoing presence of Native people in today's St. Paul.

Over the last few years, local and regional organizations have increasingly recognized the rich Dakota and Ojibwe histories of the Twin Cities area through projects like the Minnesota Humanities Center's online Bdote Memory Map, which displays Dakota sites in St. Paul and the region. One important example sits underneath the Dakota burial sites of Indian Mounds Regional Park, the remnants of a cave known as Wakaŋ Tipi, the Dwelling Place of the Sacred. It is a Dakota sacred site, known for millennia as the home of a water spirit. In 1766 Jonathan Carver, a mapmaker traveling with a British exploring expedition, described the cave, and subsequent whites applied his name to it.

The cave survived years of abuse and destruction, such as when it was dammed up in 1870, its water diverted to supply a nearby soda pop enterprise. By 1886, construction for a new railroad shaved off the front section of the cliff face, eradicating much of the cave below. In 1913, a group of boosters called the Mounds Park Improvement Association tried again to resurrect the cave and transform the cavern's remnants into an electric-lit tourist attraction. They drained some water to reveal deeper sections of the cavern, but the efforts failed to attract an audience.

Today, Wakaŋ Tipi and the wetland by the bluff sit in the Bruce Vento Nature Sanctuary, a short walk from downtown St. Paul. The Lower Phalen Creek Project, a nonprofit with Native staff, has organized numerous projects to reclaim and restore the area. Looking closely at the site, it's possible to imagine the transformation of the cave over the years, from sacred site to rubble to tourist attraction to town dump. Today's park, full of wetlands and prairies, still exists uneasily with the railroads and highways that surround it. Yet the prairie grasses, wetland pools, and clumps of cottonwoods give a slender glimpse of what the land might have looked like hundreds of years ago, when it was still the sacred site of a Dakota village, a place for planting, singing, praying, and hunting.

Inside Wakaŋ Tipi, about 1920

St. Paul's shifting demographics laid the foundation for a new urban identity, one that departed from the winter carnival and Lake Wobegon stories that had once been the center of the city's self-image. Both the Twin Cities in general, and St. Paul in particular, had long been seen as a predominantly white place. As the twentieth century wore on, white cultural hegemony intensified as initial differences between groups like Anglo-Saxons, Irish, Italians, and even Jewish Americans were largely erased and replaced with broader "Minnesotan" traditions and identities. Yet for those not deemed "white," segregation and structural racism widened gaps in access to jobs and housing. As the Twin Cities economy grew, these existing inequities deepened, between the city's white, Black, and Native American populations as well as newer arrivals to the metro area. Because of its smaller size and less overall wealth, this inequality has become especially visible in St. Paul. In 2019, St. Paul became a majority minority city, with white residents making up less than half the population for the first time.

While the Twin Cities often make national lists of most successful American metro areas, by the twenty-first century the Twin Cities also had some of the country's most extreme racial opportunity gaps. Disparities in wealth and education, particularly among white, Black, and Native American people, remain wider in the metro area than just about everywhere else. This ongoing injustice places additional focus on both St. Paul and Minneapolis, which are home to the vast majority of the metro's disinvested communities, termed "areas of racially concentrated poverty." Redressing these long-standing inequalities poses a regional and statewide challenge, one made more difficult by increased polarization between urban and rural Minnesota.

Within St. Paul's borders, the city remains segregated, with wealth disproportionately found in certain neighborhoods and poverty concentrated in others. This imbalance affects nearly every policy decision in the city, and questions about equity and how best to use the city's limited budget are at the forefront of policy and community conversations. With straitened budgets and stark social challenges, St. Paul's leaders have few easy choices when it comes to fostering economic growth while crafting equitable policies.

St. Paul's fiscal picture is not helped by the relatively limited tax base of its downtown, whose health has fluctuated along with the global economy. On one hand, the old downtown of department stores and skyway malls has faded. The city's last department store, Macy's (in the old Dayton's building), had been propped up by a city loan requiring it to stay open until 2013. When the loan ran out, the store predictably closed, the final falling domino for St. Paul's once-thriving downtown retail scene. At the same time, downtown struggled to attract jobs into aging office buildings. Companies like Thomson Reuters (formerly West Publishing) decamped for a suburban office park in nearby Eagan in 1992, while mergers took banking and insurance jobs out of the city. The shifting downtown fortunes limit St. Paul's tax base, particularly since the biggest employers are often tax-exempt government offices or nonprofits. The shortcoming has meant that St. Paul has had to become creative about putting together project financing, relying on tax shifts or public/private partnerships to keep funding projects like the downtown "ambassadors" or placemaking programs.

At the same time, other sectors of downtown have boomed. In 2016, developers bought the 1930s post office and remodeled it into a hotel, luxury apartments, and a restaurant. Residential buildings rose up around downtown, doubling its population in a decade. With the Minnesota Wild hockey arena on one end and CHS Field, the Saints baseball stadium, on the other, events bring thousands of people downtown each weekend to fill up the many food and drink establishments, while the Green Line light rail and other transit connections offer easy access to the rest of the region. A large mixed-use development is currently being planned for the site of the former West Publishing headquarters and Ramsey County jail. If it is built, it would revitalize downtown's commercial core while connecting downtown to the Mississippi River with a large public park built over the railroads and Shepard Road.

Elsewhere, large parts of the city have had similar new waves of growth and development, leading to the kind of housing boom not seen in generations. In the west Midway, the city's industrial center, new apartment buildings rise up amid the white-and-green warehouses and factories. Not far away, just south of University Avenue, a craft brewery occupies a long-mothballed mattress factory across the street from a massive paper recycling plant that runs twenty-four hours a day. On the West Side Flats, new apartment buildings stand next to the riverfront barge loading facility, and balconies for the new residents look out on empty lots that have been vacant since they were bulldozed by the city in the 1960s.

As St. Paul's new immigrant groups have established themselves over the years, second and third generations have likewise transformed the city's political climate. On the East Side, for example, voters have elected a growing number of Hmong men and women to the state legislature, school board, and city council. The diverse politics of the twenty-first century marked a departure from previous decades, where a more conservative approach was the norm in city hall. During the 1990s and 2000s, two different St. Paul mayors flirted with the Republican party. These days, St. Paul voters almost always elect DFL and Democratic candidates with overwhelming majorities.

Over the years, St. Paul's role as a Democratic bastion has helped the city access a good share of state and federal funding for infrastructure projects, most notably the return of rail transit to St. Paul's streets. While the loss of the once-widespread streetcar system in 1954 left a hole in the urban fabric, decades later city and regional planners began to imagine how rail transit might return in the region. After plans for the "downtown people mover" were scrapped, planners began a decades-long effort to bring light rail to St. Paul, running down University Avenue.

The idea for a light-rail system had been on the books since 1982, modeled after similar projects in San Diego and Edmonton, Alberta. In theory, a fast connection between downtown St. Paul and downtown Minneapolis via University Avenue would be the first big project, attracting business to the downtowns and connecting through the dense University of Minnesota campus. But because of funding concerns, Governor Jesse Ventura and regional planners shifted their initial plans to a more convenient right-of-way between downtown Minneapolis and the MSP airport. After the Blue Line opened in 2004, and became a transit success with high ridership, work soon began for the long-awaited University Avenue line to St. Paul.

The Central Corridor project rekindled concerns about government intervention, displacement, and gentrification. At the very least, years of construction would impact businesses along the street, especially the smaller shops owned by people of color. On top of that, initial plans called for stops to be spaced a mile apart, skipping over many of the corners in the heart of the working-class neighborhoods to speed up travel. As a result, many St. Paulites feared that the new line would be another Rondo, catering to the needs of wealthier white people to move quickly through St. Paul at the expense of folks who actually lived in the neighborhood. In response, community organizers and district councils (city-supported engagement organizations) in Frogtown, Summit-University, and Hamline-Midway neighborhoods demanded that project planners add three additional stops at Western, Victoria, and Hamline Avenues.

Changing a massive infrastructure plan is normally next to impossible, but St. Paul officials and project planners managed to find extra funding. When the line finally opened in 2014, after three years of disruptive construction, it stopped all along University Avenue's working-class intersections. To this day, the Green Line remains the region's most-used transit spine, thanks in part to the community pressure that ensured it aligned with community needs.

On its way through St. Paul, the Green Line passes a kaleidoscopic mix of restaurants, small businesses, affordable housing, and much more. At Snelling Avenue, it stops in front of Allianz Field, a Major League Soccer stadium that opened in 2019 on the site that once housed the giant streetcar shops. The home of the Minnesota United has helped catalyze construction of the first market-rate housing built in the central University Avenue area in over forty years, on the sites of an old bank and furniture store. The changing development will help alleviate a long-lasting housing shortage in St. Paul, where population growth and demand for homes has outstripped new construction for years. The challenge for city leaders will be adding new buildings and new residents to the community without disrupting or displacing the existing diverse cultures that already thrive there.

The billion-dollar Green Line transit project symbolizes St. Paul's critical role in the other huge challenge facing the Twin Cities. Climate change is a global problem that is profoundly affecting Minnesota, with winters warming particularly quickly. Taking the necessary steps to decarbonize the regional economy requires rethinking how cities are built, placing added urgency on urban transit investments and new developments in St. Paul. Particularly in a vacuum of federal policy, cities like St. Paul have been forced to lead the way on climate policy, and in 2019 the city adopted an ambitious Climate Action and Resilience Plan. Its goals call for reducing driving within St. Paul while investing in green energy and widespread efficiency measures aimed at the city's most vulnerable populations. Following through on these critical measures will mean increasing the pace and scale of change all across St. Paul, transforming the transportation network, and accommodating more growth than the city has seen in almost a century.

Work has already begun. In 2020, the city population once again passed a milestone: 310,000 people. After peaking in 1960 and slowly

Metro Transit's Green Line light-rail train at Victoria Station on University Avenue, 2014. *Courtesy Metro Transit*

declining, in the 1990s the city began growing again, and by 2020 had exceeded its previous high-water mark. The growth is due to a mix of migration, new construction around downtown, St. Anthony Park, and Highland, and infill development happening throughout the city. Many of the same sites that were once cleared of housing for parking lots or office parks are finally being reused for new and diverse purposes.

Like many American cities dealing with growth, structural racism, and wealth inequality, fortunes vary across St. Paul's landscape. In some parts of town, 150-year-old industrial areas attract warehousing jobs, some former factory sites languish, while others are being transformed by new uses. Elsewhere, the older streetcar corridors across the city continue to thrive, boasting a dizzying array of bodegas, markets, auto repair shops, corner stores, and restaurants reflecting dozens of different nationalities, languages, and cuisines. There are stark contrasts: traveling south on a street like Western Avenue, you pass alongside the duplexes lining the streets of historic Frogtown, then up into the now-thriving Cathedral Hill neighborhood around Selby Avenue. Rehabbed Victorian homes, nestled in among a thriving food and restaurant scene, stand just up the hill from public housing alongside the freeway. On the East Side, Hmong entrepreneurs have transformed an old strip mall into a huge marketplace, Hmong Village, probably the city's busiest. Nearly every day of the year, the labyrinthine market is full of people, its narrow interior passages lined with hundreds of shops, conversations and music filling the building as vendors sell cloth, dresses, clothing, toys, DVDs, medicinal herbs, and a variety of merchandise.

St. Paul is full of similar contrasts, part of an American society and economy reaching levels of inequality not seen for a century. Today, the conflicting perspectives about St. Paul's future can be seen in the transformation taking place in the prosperous, middle-class Highland Park neighborhood, on the southwest edge of the city. In 2011, the final Ranger pickup truck rolled off the Ford assembly line at the sprawling ninety-year-old factory. Throughout its lifespan, the Twin Cities Ford Plant was one of the most successful plants in company history.

But with global economic disruption, the company closed the site after years of dwindling projections, taking well-paying union jobs out of St. Paul.

The only good news was that, unlike every other shuttered car factory in the country, Ford did not simply sell the land. Instead, the company spent years cleaning up the soil and preparing the site for redevelopment. Just as had been the case when the factory was first pitched, St. Paul leaders were eager to jump in and aid Ford in the cause. City officials worked with the company to plan an ambitious redevelopment, touring Europe to find examples of how to build a sustainable, walkable, urban community on the 122-acre site.

In 2017, city planners proposed a high-density, transit-oriented development at the old factory site that would mix housing with offices and retail along the Mississippi River. The plan called for four thousand new market-rate and affordable homes, as well as a mix of retail and jobs along Ford Parkway. For some people in the neighborhood, the density of the proposal was unsettling, and concerns about traffic and parking began to dominate community meetings and letters to the editor. However, younger environmental and housing advocates organized in support of the plans, pointing to the need for new housing in a city where rents and prices were rising fast. For months, competing lawn signs appeared along the streets of St. Paul—red ones saying, "Stop the Ford Plan" and green ones saying, "Say Yes to the Ford Site." Church basements and rec centers throughout Highland hosted heated community meetings that did not seem to resolve the debate.

The city election of 2017 settled the matter. In a citywide vote, Melvin Carter III, son of a Black St. Paul police officer and a current Ramsey County commissioner, and grandson of a Rondo neighborhood musician and Red Cap porter, was elected mayor by a two-to-one margin. Importantly, Carter had campaigned in support of the density in the new Highland community. By 2020, the cleanup of the contaminated factory site was complete, and the first of thousands of homes of the new community, now dubbed by the developers Highland Bridge, were under construction. Within a few years, thousands of new people will be living in the neighborhood, creating an uncertain future for a city that remains full of promise.

When the neighborhood does finally flourish, it will surely have its own farmers market, because few things symbolize the vitality and diversity of St. Paul better than the seasonal markets that sprout in parking lots in every corner of town. To take just one example: Hmongtown, St. Paul's other large Hmong marketplace just northwest of the state capitol, in the large buildings of a repurposed lumberyard, has a farmers market every day in summer. The back of the large complex is lined with tents underneath which Hmong vendors sell fresh produce: fruits, vegetables, herbs, and every other imaginable local crop. It's just one of dozens of markets scattered around town, places where people from all parts of the city come to find food and community.

Large as they are, the rows of vendors at the tables in Hmongtown pale in size compared to the city's oldest and largest farmers market, which takes up a full city block in the heart of historic Lowertown. The downtown market began in 1902 at Tenth and Jackson, before it was displaced in 1982 due to downtown construction. Since the very beginning, the market has connected St. Paul's urban residents to the thriving farms within fifty miles, providing fresh produce in the summer and dairy and meat during the long winter months. Each Saturday and Sunday from late spring until fall, vendors pile produce and wares onto long lines of tables that sit underneath the overhangs, and folks come from all over the metro to walk along the brick paths that run between the vendors.

As Hmong writer Kao Kalia Yang notes, the farmers themselves reflect the city's diverse history, with Hmong farmers rubbing elbows with family farmers descended from the region's first European growers. Elsewhere in the city, farmers markets pop up in any extra space available, behind a Catholic school on Lexington Parkway, in the parking lot of a strip mall on University and Dale, alongside the brewery in St. Anthony Park's industrial area, on the East Side next to the food trucks of White Bear Avenue. They are everywhere you find a mix of St. Paul people, some old, some young, some newcomers, some going back generations.

These days, St. Paul boasts rich tradition and possibility, and it is changing faster than it has in many years. There are millions of stories to tell about St. Paul, histories and people and places and perspectives that lie outside any one narrative. It is a city that can foster frustration and fealty, inspire intense devotion or eye rolling in equal measure.

In fundamental ways, it's impossible to reconcile St. Paul's history with the Dakota world that preceded it and still remains alive in this place near where the rivers meet. Likewise, the stories of the city's wealth, its monuments, and its many triumphs must never conceal the exploitation that lies at their root. So many of St. Paul's accomplishments have been accompanied by injustice, and recognizing these truths is the fundamental task for creating a more equitable future. For this reason, learning the complicated history of the city is critically important. What does it mean to live in this particular place, along this particular

Phoua Hang, a founding member of the Hmong American Farmers Association, sells produce at the St. Paul Farmers' Market, October 2015. *Mike Hazard*

river, in this part of the world? The uneven geography of St. Paul is best understood from contrasting perspectives. Solving its problems requires learning to live in a city where futures are intertwined. Uniquely positioned on the Mississippi, and at the intersection of key challenges facing both the country and the region, St. Paul is poised to once more lead the way.

For Further Reading

Most of the chapters in this book rely on these excellent books, which provide both general background and in-depth treatment of specific periods: Virginia Brainard Kunz, *Saint Paul: The First 150 Years* (St. Paul: St. Paul Foundation, 1991); J. Fletcher Williams, *A History of the City of St. Paul to 1875* (1876; repr., St. Paul: MNHS, 1983); Mary Lethert Wingerd, *Claiming the City: Politics, Faith, and the Power of Place in St. Paul* (Ithaca, NY: Cornell University Press, 2001) and *North Country: The Making of Minnesota* (Minneapolis: University of Minnesota Press, 2010).

Readers interested in knowing more about St. Paul history will find much of interest in the sources listed below, which are specific to each chapter. These notes also provide sources for quotations.

1. Naming

Rhoda R. Gilman, *Henry Hastings Sibley: Divided Heart* (St. Paul: MNHS Press, 2004); William D. Green, *A Peculiar Imbalance: The Fall and Rise of Racial Equality in Minnesota* (St. Paul: MNHS Press, 2009); Gwen Westerman and Bruce White, *Mni Sota Makoce: The Land of the Dakota* (St. Paul: MNHS Press, 2012).

Quotations: p. 8, 10, "a remarkable cave": Jonathan Carver, *Three Years Travels through the Interior Parts of North-America* (Philadelphia: Key and Simpson, 1796), 40; p. 9, "The French—and the British and Americans who followed": Wingerd, *North Country*, 42; p. 17, "doomed . . . to disappear": Williams, *History of St. Paul*, 40; p. 20, "ever after . . . were good friends": Green, *Peculiar Imbalance*, 35; p. 20, "some half dozen decayed . . . hovels": Harriet E. Bishop, *Floral Home, or First Years of Minnesota: Early Sketches, Later Settlements, and Further Developments* (New York: Sheldon, Blakeman and Company, 1857), 47.

2. Dispossession

Gary Clayton Anderson, *Little Crow: Spokesman for the Sioux* (St. Paul: MNHS Press, 1986); Nick Estes, *Our History Is the Future: Standing Rock versus the Dakota Access Pipeline* (N.p.: Verso, 2019); Green, *Peculiar Imbalance*.

Quotations: p. 25, "Saint Paul['s] . . . new frame buildings": E. S. Seymour, *Sketches of Minnesota, the New England of the West* (New York: Harper, 1850), 94; p. 25, "the town's greatest holiday": quoted in Jocelyn Wills, *Boosters, Hustlers, and Speculators: Entrepreneurial Culture and the Rise of Minneapolis and St. Paul, 1849–1883* (St. Paul: MNHS Press, 2005), 43; p. 28, "One would suppose by the promises" and "My ears at every turn": Williams, *History of St. Paul*, 271–72, 332; p. 32, "the dignity and rules": Wingerd, *North Country*, 251; p. 32, "the jug of empire": Mark Twain, *Life on the Mississippi* (New York: Grossett and Dunlap, 1917), 491; p. 32, "On the night of the repeal": Bishop, *Floral Home*, 111; p. 33, "as among our most 'solid'": Williams, *History of St. Paul*, 271; p. 33, "I can't tell how many slaves we got away": Wingerd, *North Country*, 244; p. 34, "the police were very much alarmed": Green, *Peculiar Imbalance*, 130; p. 35, "Emigration was pouring in": Williams, *History of St. Paul*, 354; p. 38, "a war of extermination": *St. Paul Press*, August 22, 1862, quoted in Emily Rankin Wardrop, "'All the Women . . . Were Violated in This Way': Rhetoric, Rape, and Memory in the Dakota War" (PhD diss., University of Oklahoma, 2015), 17; p. 38, "open letter from the citizens": Wingerd, *North Country*, 336.

3. Boomtown

John W. Diers and Aaron Isaacs, *Twin Cities by Trolley: The Streetcar Era in Minneapolis and St. Paul* (Minneapolis: University of Minnesota Press, 2007); Wills, *Boosters, Hustlers, and Speculators*.

Quotations: p. 45, "St. Paul is a wonderful town": Twain, *Life on the Mississippi*, 488, 490; p. 61, "the claws of class": Patricial Hampl, introduction to *The St. Paul Stories of F. Scott Fitzgerald*, ed. Dave Page (St. Paul: Borealis Books, 2004), xv.

4. Overshadowed

Wingerd, *Claiming the City.*

Quotations: p. 63, 64, "another Siberia" and "every color of the rainbow": Robert A. Olson, "'Another Siberia, Unfit for Human Habitation'? St. Paul's Super Ice Palaces, 1886, 1887, 1888," *Ramsey County History* 52 (Winter 2018): 3, 6; p. 68, "Scheme to Swell the Population" and "Dastardly Outrage Committed": Virginia Brainard Kunz, "An Excess of Zeal and Boosterism—Few Holds Barred in Twin Cities Rivalries," *Ramsey County History* 25 (Summer 1990): 5; p. 72, "midnight orgies": quoted in Richard Chin, "'Midnight Orgies' Ended St. Paddy's Day Parade," *St. Paul Pioneer Press*, March 16, 2016; p. 73, "in all my life": quoted in Tamara C. Truer, "Eugene V. Debs, James J. Hill and the Great Northern Railway's Strike of 1894," *Ramsey County History* 25 (Spring 1990): 23; p. 74, "open shop capital of America": Wingerd, *Claiming the City*, 91; p. 75, "the interdependence of business and labor": Wingerd, *Claiming the City*, 97.

5. Wheeling and Dealing

Gareth Hiebert, multiple works, including *Once Upon a Towne* (St. Paul: North Central Publishing Co., 1959) and *Oliver's Towns* (St. Paul: Pogo Press, 2000); William Hoffman, multiple works, including *Those Were the Days* (Minneapolis: T. S. Denison, 1957) and *West Side Story II* (St. Paul: North Central Publishing Co., 1981); Paul Maccabee, *John Dillinger Slept Here: A Crooks' Tour of Crime and Corruption in St. Paul, 1920–1936* (St. Paul: MNHS Press, 1995); Brian McMahon, *Ford Century in Minnesota* (Minneapolis: University of Minnesota Press, 2016); Gordon Parks, *A Choice of Weapons* (New York: Harper & Row, 1966; repr., St. Paul: MNHS Press, 1986).

Quotations: p. 81, "If they behaved themselves": quoted in Maccabee, *Dillinger*, 9; p. 81, "As a matter of fact, the Ford hydroelectric": McMahon,

Ford Century, 100; p. 87, "My father was the political king": Hiebert, *Oliver's Towns,* 50; p. 87, "The Empire Builder ran from Chicago": Melvin Whitfield Carter Jr., *Diesel Heart: An Autobiography* (St. Paul: MNHS Press, 2019), 10; p. 91, "I couldn't imagine such financial disaster": Parks, *Choice of Weapons,* 55; p. 93, "I didn't know I had an enemy": quoted in Maccabee, *Dillinger,* 2; p. 95, "lost his topper": quoted in Maccabee, *Dillinger,* 121.

6. Bulldozer

Alan A. Altshuler, *A Report on Politics in St. Paul, Minnesota* (Cambridge, MA: Joint Center for Urban Studies of the Massachusetts Institute of Technology and Harvard University, 1959) and *The City Planning Process: A Political Analysis* (Ithaca, NY: Cornell University Press, 1965); Kate Cavett and David V. Taylor, *Voices of Rondo: Oral Histories of Saint Paul's Historic Black Community* (Minneapolis: Syren Book Co., 2005; repr., University of Minnesota Press, 2017); Hiebert, *Once Upon a Towne* and *Oliver's Towns*; David V. Taylor, "Pilgrim's Progress: Black St. Paul and the Making of an Urban Ghetto" (PhD diss., University of Minnesota, 1977); Dionicio Valdés, *Barrios Norteños: St. Paul and Midwestern Mexican Communities in the 20th Century* (Austin: University of Texas Press: 2000).

Quotations: p. 101, "Did you ever watch": letter written to Gareth Hiebert, October 8, 1958, quoted in Hiebert, *Once Upon a Towne,* 17; p. 103, "Close up, the city is lines of cars": Hiebert, *Oliver's Towns,* 1; p. 106, "[St. Paul] should be made as attractive": Altshuler, *Report on Politics,* 1:8; p. 107, "The district . . . is very hilly": Robert K. Nelson, LaDale Winling, Richard Marciano, Nathan Connolly, et al., "Mapping Inequality: Redlining in New Deal America," American Panorama, ed. Robert K. Nelson and Edward L. Ayers, https://dsl.richmond.edu/panorama/redlining/#loc=11/44.938/-93.262&city=st.-paul-mn; p. 108, "Long dominated by Minneapolis": reprinted in *Minneapolis Morning Tribune,* July 7, 1959, 4; p. 108, "There isn't much left": Hiebert, *Once Upon a Towne,* 29; p. 109, "a ghetto district": Nelson, et al., "Mapping Inequality"; p. 110, "the 'flats' if properly treated": Carol Aronovici, *Housing Conditions in the City of*

Saint Paul: Report Presented to the Housing Commission of the St. Paul Association (St. Paul: Amherst H. Wilder Charity, 1917), 11; p. 111, "'urban renewal' in the barrio": Valdés, *Barrios Norteños*, 175; p. 117, "American freeways tended to twist": Peter Callaghan, "Reconciling with Rondo," *MinnPost*, October 14, 2016.

7. Resilience

Carter, *Diesel Heart*; William Swanson, *Black White Blue: The Assassination of Patrolman Sackett* (St. Paul: Borealis Books, 2012); Biloine W. Young and David A. Lanegran, *Grand Avenue: The Renaissance of an Urban Street* (St. Cloud, MN: North Star Press, 1997).

Quotations: p. 119, "Such snug urban enclaves": Hampl, *The Florist's Daughter* (Boston: Mariner Books, 2009), 122; p. 129, "When I was growing up": Carter, *Diesel Heart*, 203; p. 131, "virtually no patronage": Altshuler, *Report on Politics*, 2:2.

8. Renaissance

Donald Empson and Kathleen M. Vadnais, *The Street Where You Live: A Guide to the Place Names of St. Paul* (Minneapolis: University of Minnesota Press, 2006); Paul Hillmer, *A People's History of the Hmong* (St. Paul: MNHS Press, 2010).

Quotations: p. 139, "When I stepped close": Kao Kalia Yang, "Farmers Market Memories," in Hannah Hayes, *Wildsam Field Guides: Twin Cities* (Austin, TX: Wildsam Field Guides, [2020]), 107–8; p. 140, "When we arrived here": Hillmer, *People's History*, 245; p. 140, "We couldn't understand the language": Hillmer, *People's History*, 242; p. 142, "Diversity is coming to be looked on": Alice L. Sickels, *Around the World in St. Paul* (Minneapolis: University of Minnesota Press, 1945), 190; p. 143, "I turned a corner": Wing Young Huie, *Frogtown: Photographs and Conversations in an Urban Neighborhood* (St. Paul: MNHS Press, 1996), 4.

Acknowledgments

This book is dedicated to my father, Craig Lindeke, who instilled in me his curmudgeonly love for St. Paul idiosyncrasy. As I was writing this book, during the COVID pandemic, my dad died of heart failure at a St. Paul hospital. Months later, in the very same hospital, I began writing this acknowledgment on the day my daughter Ruth was born. As my wife's labor began, I spied the First National Bank's "1st" sign through a crack in the curtains, reminding me that, even in our most stressful times, St. Paul bridges the past and future. It remains, for me and so many others, a place to call home.

I am grateful for my enthusiastic and experienced editor, Ann Regan, who managed to drop off all the research materials I needed for this book despite the plague, and who worked tirelessly to make this book seem better than it deserves. Thanks to Jim and Roxanne, who years ago shared with me their stories and wisdom at the shore of Wakaŋ Tipi, and all the other Indigenous scholars and elders who have helped people like me begin to rethink how I view this place. Thanks to the dogged St. Paul historians who have documented this city's unique history over the years, whether on Facebook or in the many well-researched articles and books that survive. Thanks to all the Twin Cities librarians—especially Peter—who keep their archives in order. Thanks to Ella, Sara, and Kate for providing rare summertime cabin camaraderie during a pandemic. I owe a great debt to my West Side writers group, Sue, Anne, and Anna, for their edits and support. Finally, thanks to my wife, Emily, who patiently gave me space to work and even found time to read some chapters, despite the nonstop demands of her job.

Index

Italicized page numbers indicate an illustration or its caption.